C-2072   CAREER EXAMINATION SERIES

*This is your
PASSBOOK for...*

Director of School Facilities and Operations

*Test Preparation Study Guide
Questions & Answers*

COPYRIGHT NOTICE

This book is SOLELY intended for, is sold ONLY to, and its use is RESTRICTED to individual, bona fide applicants or candidates who qualify by virtue of having seriously filed applications for appropriate license, certificate, professional and/or promotional advancement, higher school matriculation, scholarship, or other legitimate requirements of education and/or governmental authorities.

This book is NOT intended for use, class instruction, tutoring, training, duplication, copying, reprinting, excerption, or adaptation, etc., by:

1) Other publishers
2) Proprietors and/or Instructors of "Coaching" and/or Preparatory Courses
3) Personnel and/or Training Divisions of commercial, industrial, and governmental organizations
4) Schools, colleges, or universities and/or their departments and staffs, including teachers and other personnel
5) Testing Agencies or Bureaus
6) Study groups which seek by the purchase of a single volume to copy and/or duplicate and/or adapt this material for use by the group as a whole without having purchased individual volumes for each of the members of the group
7) Et al.

Such persons would be in violation of appropriate Federal and State statutes.

PROVISION OF LICENSING AGREEMENTS – Recognized educational, commercial, industrial, and governmental institutions and organizations, and others legitimately engaged in educational pursuits, including training, testing, and measurement activities, may address request for a licensing agreement to the copyright owners, who will determine whether, and under what conditions, including fees and charges, the materials in this book may be used them. In other words, a licensing facility exists for the legitimate use of the material in this book on other than an individual basis. However, it is asseverated and affirmed here that the material in this book CANNOT be used without the receipt of the express permission of such a licensing agreement from the Publishers. Inquiries re licensing should be addressed to the company, attention rights and permissions department.

All rights reserved, including the right of reproduction in whole or in part, in any form or by any means, electronic or mechanical, including photocopying, recording, or by any information storage and retrieval system, without permission in writing from the Publisher.

Copyright © 2024 by
National Learning Corporation

212 Michael Drive, Syosset, NY 11791
(516) 921-8888 • www.passbooks.com
E-mail: info@passbooks.com

PASSBOOK® SERIES

THE *PASSBOOK® SERIES* has been created to prepare applicants and candidates for the ultimate academic battlefield – the examination room.

At some time in our lives, each and every one of us may be required to take an examination – for validation, matriculation, admission, qualification, registration, certification, or licensure.

Based on the assumption that every applicant or candidate has met the basic formal educational standards, has taken the required number of courses, and read the necessary texts, the *PASSBOOK® SERIES* furnishes the one special preparation which may assure passing with confidence, instead of failing with insecurity. Examination questions – together with answers – are furnished as the basic vehicle for study so that the mysteries of the examination and its compounding difficulties may be eliminated or diminished by a sure method.

This book is meant to help you pass your examination provided that you qualify and are serious in your objective.

The entire field is reviewed through the huge store of content information which is succinctly presented through a provocative and challenging approach – the question-and-answer method.

A climate of success is established by furnishing the correct answers at the end of each test.

You soon learn to recognize types of questions, forms of questions, and patterns of questioning. You may even begin to anticipate expected outcomes.

You perceive that many questions are repeated or adapted so that you can gain acute insights, which may enable you to score many sure points.

You learn how to confront new questions, or types of questions, and to attack them confidently and work out the correct answers.

You note objectives and emphases, and recognize pitfalls and dangers, so that you may make positive educational adjustments.

Moreover, you are kept fully informed in relation to new concepts, methods, practices, and directions in the field.

You discover that you are actually taking the examination all the time: you are preparing for the examination by "taking" an examination, not by reading extraneous and/or supererogatory textbooks.

In short, this PASSBOOK®, used directedly, should be an important factor in helping you to pass your test.

DIRECTOR OF SCHOOL FACILITIES AND OPERATIONS

DUTIES
Has charge of school district maintenance and operations activities; plans, implements, coordinates and supervises a program of buildings, grounds and facilities maintenance and operation for a school district; performs related duties as required.

EXAMPLES OF TYPICAL TASKS
Plans, schedules and supervises maintenance and repair activities for school district buildings, grounds and equipment which also includes a program of preventive maintenance; plans and supervises cleaning activities in each building through subordinate senior custodians; schedules and determines work priorities with the senior custodian; conducts periodic inspections of the condition of the buildings and equipment including boilers and heating and ventilation equipment to ascertain maintenance needs and to ensure compliance with work and safety standards; develops and implements a preventive maintenance program designed to retain buildings, grounds and equipment in safe operating condition; makes recommendations and cost estimates for needed contractual maintenance work; solicits bids from vendors for contracted maintenance work; assists in planning and implementing major renovations to heating and ventilation systems; supervises snow removal, lawn care and athletic field preparation activities; makes recommendations to school officials on maintenance, repair and operational needs; prepares budget for school district cleaning and maintenance operations; interviews and makes recommendations for appointment of custodial and maintenance operations; maintains materials for the implementation of requirements under the Right-to-Know Law; and ensures that school district is in compliance with state and federal regulations and requirements regarding asbestos control and removal.

SCOPE OF THE EXAMINATION
The multiple-choice test will cover knowledge, skills and abilities in such areas as:

1. Building and grounds maintenance and repair;
2. Building trades including mechanical and electrical;
3. Operation and maintenance of building heating and ventilation systems;
4. Work scheduling;
5. Interpretation of plans and specifications and preparation of estimates; and
6. Administrative supervision.

HOW TO TAKE A TEST

I. YOU MUST PASS AN EXAMINATION

A. WHAT EVERY CANDIDATE SHOULD KNOW

Examination applicants often ask us for help in preparing for the written test. What can I study in advance? What kinds of questions will be asked? How will the test be given? How will the papers be graded?

As an applicant for a civil service examination, you may be wondering about some of these things. Our purpose here is to suggest effective methods of advance study and to describe civil service examinations.

Your chances for success on this examination can be increased if you know how to prepare. Those "pre-examination jitters" can be reduced if you know what to expect. You can even experience an adventure in good citizenship if you know why civil service exams are given.

B. WHY ARE CIVIL SERVICE EXAMINATIONS GIVEN?

Civil service examinations are important to you in two ways. As a citizen, you want public jobs filled by employees who know how to do their work. As a job seeker, you want a fair chance to compete for that job on an equal footing with other candidates. The best-known means of accomplishing this two-fold goal is the competitive examination.

Exams are widely publicized throughout the nation. They may be administered for jobs in federal, state, city, municipal, town or village governments or agencies.

Any citizen may apply, with some limitations, such as the age or residence of applicants. Your experience and education may be reviewed to see whether you meet the requirements for the particular examination. When these requirements exist, they are reasonable and applied consistently to all applicants. Thus, a competitive examination may cause you some uneasiness now, but it is your privilege and safeguard.

C. HOW ARE CIVIL SERVICE EXAMS DEVELOPED?

Examinations are carefully written by trained technicians who are specialists in the field known as "psychological measurement," in consultation with recognized authorities in the field of work that the test will cover. These experts recommend the subject matter areas or skills to be tested; only those knowledges or skills important to your success on the job are included. The most reliable books and source materials available are used as references. Together, the experts and technicians judge the difficulty level of the questions.

Test technicians know how to phrase questions so that the problem is clearly stated. Their ethics do not permit "trick" or "catch" questions. Questions may have been tried out on sample groups, or subjected to statistical analysis, to determine their usefulness.

Written tests are often used in combination with performance tests, ratings of training and experience, and oral interviews. All of these measures combine to form the best-known means of finding the right person for the right job.

II. HOW TO PASS THE WRITTEN TEST

A. NATURE OF THE EXAMINATION

To prepare intelligently for civil service examinations, you should know how they differ from school examinations you have taken. In school you were assigned certain definite pages to read or subjects to cover. The examination questions were quite detailed and usually emphasized memory. Civil service exams, on the other hand, try to discover your present ability to perform the duties of a position, plus your potentiality to learn these duties. In other words, a civil service exam attempts to predict how successful you will be. Questions cover such a broad area that they cannot be as minute and detailed as school exam questions.

In the public service similar kinds of work, or positions, are grouped together in one "class." This process is known as *position-classification*. All the positions in a class are paid according to the salary range for that class. One class title covers all of these positions, and they are all tested by the same examination.

B. FOUR BASIC STEPS

1) Study the announcement

How, then, can you know what subjects to study? Our best answer is: "Learn as much as possible about the class of positions for which you've applied." The exam will test the knowledge, skills and abilities needed to do the work.

Your most valuable source of information about the position you want is the official exam announcement. This announcement lists the training and experience qualifications. Check these standards and apply only if you come reasonably close to meeting them.

The brief description of the position in the examination announcement offers some clues to the subjects which will be tested. Think about the job itself. Review the duties in your mind. Can you perform them, or are there some in which you are rusty? Fill in the blank spots in your preparation.

Many jurisdictions preview the written test in the exam announcement by including a section called "Knowledge and Abilities Required," "Scope of the Examination," or some similar heading. Here you will find out specifically what fields will be tested.

2) Review your own background

Once you learn in general what the position is all about, and what you need to know to do the work, ask yourself which subjects you already know fairly well and which need improvement. You may wonder whether to concentrate on improving your strong areas or on building some background in your fields of weakness. When the announcement has specified "some knowledge" or "considerable knowledge," or has used adjectives like "beginning principles of..." or "advanced ... methods," you can get a clue as to the number and difficulty of questions to be asked in any given field. More questions, and hence broader coverage, would be included for those subjects which are more important in the work. Now weigh your strengths and weaknesses against the job requirements and prepare accordingly.

3) Determine the level of the position

Another way to tell how intensively you should prepare is to understand the level of the job for which you are applying. Is it the entering level? In other words, is this the position in which beginners in a field of work are hired? Or is it an intermediate or advanced level? Sometimes this is indicated by such words as "Junior" or "Senior" in the class title. Other jurisdictions use Roman numerals to designate the level – Clerk I, Clerk II, for example. The word "Supervisor" sometimes appears in the title. If the level is not indicated by the title, check the description of duties. Will you be working under very close supervision, or will you have responsibility for independent decisions in this work?

4) Choose appropriate study materials

Now that you know the subjects to be examined and the relative amount of each subject to be covered, you can choose suitable study materials. For beginning level jobs, or even advanced ones, if you have a pronounced weakness in some aspect of your training, read a modern, standard textbook in that field. Be sure it is up to date and has general coverage. Such books are normally available at your library, and the librarian will be glad to help you locate one. For entry-level positions, questions of appropriate difficulty are chosen – neither highly advanced questions, nor those too simple. Such questions require careful thought but not advanced training.

If the position for which you are applying is technical or advanced, you will read more advanced, specialized material. If you are already familiar with the basic principles of your field, elementary textbooks would waste your time. Concentrate on advanced textbooks and technical periodicals. Think through the concepts and review difficult problems in your field.

These are all general sources. You can get more ideas on your own initiative, following these leads. For example, training manuals and publications of the government agency which employs workers in your field can be useful, particularly for technical and professional positions. A letter or visit to the government department involved may result in more specific study suggestions, and certainly will provide you with a more definite idea of the exact nature of the position you are seeking.

III. KINDS OF TESTS

Tests are used for purposes other than measuring knowledge and ability to perform specified duties. For some positions, it is equally important to test ability to make adjustments to new situations or to profit from training. In others, basic mental abilities not dependent on information are essential. Questions which test these things may not appear as pertinent to the duties of the position as those which test for knowledge and information. Yet they are often highly important parts of a fair examination. For very general questions, it is almost impossible to help you direct your study efforts. What we can do is to point out some of the more common of these general abilities needed in public service positions and describe some typical questions.

1) General information

Broad, general information has been found useful for predicting job success in some kinds of work. This is tested in a variety of ways, from vocabulary lists to questions about current events. Basic background in some field of work, such as sociology or economics, may be sampled in a group of questions. Often these are principles which have become familiar to most persons through exposure rather than through formal training. It is difficult to advise you how to study for these questions; being alert to the world around you is our best suggestion.

2) Verbal ability

An example of an ability needed in many positions is verbal or language ability. Verbal ability is, in brief, the ability to use and understand words. Vocabulary and grammar tests are typical measures of this ability. Reading comprehension or paragraph interpretation questions are common in many kinds of civil service tests. You are given a paragraph of written material and asked to find its central meaning.

3) Numerical ability

Number skills can be tested by the familiar arithmetic problem, by checking paired lists of numbers to see which are alike and which are different, or by interpreting charts and graphs. In the latter test, a graph may be printed in the test booklet which you are asked to use as the basis for answering questions.

4) Observation

A popular test for law-enforcement positions is the observation test. A picture is shown to you for several minutes, then taken away. Questions about the picture test your ability to observe both details and larger elements.

5) Following directions

In many positions in the public service, the employee must be able to carry out written instructions dependably and accurately. You may be given a chart with several columns, each column listing a variety of information. The questions require you to carry out directions involving the information given in the chart.

6) Skills and aptitudes

Performance tests effectively measure some manual skills and aptitudes. When the skill is one in which you are trained, such as typing or shorthand, you can practice. These tests are often very much like those given in business school or high school courses. For many of the other skills and aptitudes, however, no short-time preparation can be made. Skills and abilities natural to you or that you have developed throughout your lifetime are being tested.

Many of the general questions just described provide all the data needed to answer the questions and ask you to use your reasoning ability to find the answers. Your best preparation for these tests, as well as for tests of facts and ideas, is to be at your physical and mental best. You, no doubt, have your own methods of getting into an exam-taking mood and keeping "in shape." The next section lists some ideas on this subject.

IV. KINDS OF QUESTIONS

Only rarely is the "essay" question, which you answer in narrative form, used in civil service tests. Civil service tests are usually of the short-answer type. Full instructions for answering these questions will be given to you at the examination. But in case this is your first experience with short-answer questions and separate answer sheets, here is what you need to know:

1) Multiple-choice Questions

Most popular of the short-answer questions is the "multiple choice" or "best answer" question. It can be used, for example, to test for factual knowledge, ability to solve problems or judgment in meeting situations found at work.

A multiple-choice question is normally one of three types—
- It can begin with an incomplete statement followed by several possible endings. You are to find the one ending which *best* completes the statement, although some of the others may not be entirely wrong.
- It can also be a complete statement in the form of a question which is answered by choosing one of the statements listed.

- It can be in the form of a problem – again you select the best answer.

Here is an example of a multiple-choice question with a discussion which should give you some clues as to the method for choosing the right answer:

When an employee has a complaint about his assignment, the action which will *best* help him overcome his difficulty is to
- A. discuss his difficulty with his coworkers
- B. take the problem to the head of the organization
- C. take the problem to the person who gave him the assignment
- D. say nothing to anyone about his complaint

In answering this question, you should study each of the choices to find which is best. Consider choice "A" – Certainly an employee may discuss his complaint with fellow employees, but no change or improvement can result, and the complaint remains unresolved. Choice "B" is a poor choice since the head of the organization probably does not know what assignment you have been given, and taking your problem to him is known as "going over the head" of the supervisor. The supervisor, or person who made the assignment, is the person who can clarify it or correct any injustice. Choice "C" is, therefore, correct. To say nothing, as in choice "D," is unwise. Supervisors have and interest in knowing the problems employees are facing, and the employee is seeking a solution to his problem.

2) True/False Questions

The "true/false" or "right/wrong" form of question is sometimes used. Here a complete statement is given. Your job is to decide whether the statement is right or wrong.

SAMPLE: A roaming cell-phone call to a nearby city costs less than a non-roaming call to a distant city.

This statement is wrong, or false, since roaming calls are more expensive.

This is not a complete list of all possible question forms, although most of the others are variations of these common types. You will always get complete directions for answering questions. Be sure you understand *how* to mark your answers – ask questions until you do.

V. RECORDING YOUR ANSWERS

Computer terminals are used more and more today for many different kinds of exams.

For an examination with very few applicants, you may be told to record your answers in the test booklet itself. Separate answer sheets are much more common. If this separate answer sheet is to be scored by machine – and this is often the case – it is highly important that you mark your answers correctly in order to get credit.

An electronic scoring machine is often used in civil service offices because of the speed with which papers can be scored. Machine-scored answer sheets must be marked with a pencil, which will be given to you. This pencil has a high graphite content which responds to the electronic scoring machine. As a matter of fact, stray dots may register as answers, so do not let your pencil rest on the answer sheet while you are pondering the correct answer. Also, if your pencil lead breaks or is otherwise defective, ask for another.

Since the answer sheet will be dropped in a slot in the scoring machine, be careful not to bend the corners or get the paper crumpled.

The answer sheet normally has five vertical columns of numbers, with 30 numbers to a column. These numbers correspond to the question numbers in your test booklet. After each number, going across the page are four or five pairs of dotted lines. These short dotted lines have small letters or numbers above them. The first two pairs may also have a "T" or "F" above the letters. This indicates that the first two pairs only are to be used if the questions are of the true-false type. If the questions are multiple choice, disregard the "T" and "F" and pay attention only to the small letters or numbers.

Answer your questions in the manner of the sample that follows:

32. The largest city in the United States is
    A. Washington, D.C.
    B. New York City
    C. Chicago
    D. Detroit
    E. San Francisco

1) Choose the answer you think is best. (New York City is the largest, so "B" is correct.)
2) Find the row of dotted lines numbered the same as the question you are answering. (Find row number 32)
3) Find the pair of dotted lines corresponding to the answer. (Find the pair of lines under the mark "B.")
4) Make a solid black mark between the dotted lines.

VI. BEFORE THE TEST

Common sense will help you find procedures to follow to get ready for an examination. Too many of us, however, overlook these sensible measures. Indeed, nervousness and fatigue have been found to be the most serious reasons why applicants fail to do their best on civil service tests. Here is a list of reminders:

- Begin your preparation early – Don't wait until the last minute to go scurrying around for books and materials or to find out what the position is all about.
- Prepare continuously – An hour a night for a week is better than an all-night cram session. This has been definitely established. What is more, a night a week for a month will return better dividends than crowding your study into a shorter period of time.
- Locate the place of the exam – You have been sent a notice telling you when and where to report for the examination. If the location is in a different town or otherwise unfamiliar to you, it would be well to inquire the best route and learn something about the building.
- Relax the night before the test – Allow your mind to rest. Do not study at all that night. Plan some mild recreation or diversion; then go to bed early and get a good night's sleep.
- Get up early enough to make a leisurely trip to the place for the test – This way unforeseen events, traffic snarls, unfamiliar buildings, etc. will not upset you.
- Dress comfortably – A written test is not a fashion show. You will be known by number and not by name, so wear something comfortable.

- Leave excess paraphernalia at home – Shopping bags and odd bundles will get in your way. You need bring only the items mentioned in the official notice you received; usually everything you need is provided. Do not bring reference books to the exam. They will only confuse those last minutes and be taken away from you when in the test room.
- Arrive somewhat ahead of time – If because of transportation schedules you must get there very early, bring a newspaper or magazine to take your mind off yourself while waiting.
- Locate the examination room – When you have found the proper room, you will be directed to the seat or part of the room where you will sit. Sometimes you are given a sheet of instructions to read while you are waiting. Do not fill out any forms until you are told to do so; just read them and be prepared.
- Relax and prepare to listen to the instructions
- If you have any physical problem that may keep you from doing your best, be sure to tell the test administrator. If you are sick or in poor health, you really cannot do your best on the exam. You can come back and take the test some other time.

VII. AT THE TEST

The day of the test is here and you have the test booklet in your hand. The temptation to get going is very strong. Caution! There is more to success than knowing the right answers. You must know how to identify your papers and understand variations in the type of short-answer question used in this particular examination. Follow these suggestions for maximum results from your efforts:

1) Cooperate with the monitor

The test administrator has a duty to create a situation in which you can be as much at ease as possible. He will give instructions, tell you when to begin, check to see that you are marking your answer sheet correctly, and so on. He is not there to guard you, although he will see that your competitors do not take unfair advantage. He wants to help you do your best.

2) Listen to all instructions

Don't jump the gun! Wait until you understand all directions. In most civil service tests you get more time than you need to answer the questions. So don't be in a hurry. Read each word of instructions until you clearly understand the meaning. Study the examples, listen to all announcements and follow directions. Ask questions if you do not understand what to do.

3) Identify your papers

Civil service exams are usually identified by number only. You will be assigned a number; you must not put your name on your test papers. Be sure to copy your number correctly. Since more than one exam may be given, copy your exact examination title.

4) Plan your time

Unless you are told that a test is a "speed" or "rate of work" test, speed itself is usually not important. Time enough to answer all the questions will be provided, but this does not mean that you have all day. An overall time limit has been set. Divide the total time (in minutes) by the number of questions to determine the approximate time you have for each question.

5) Do not linger over difficult questions

If you come across a difficult question, mark it with a paper clip (useful to have along) and come back to it when you have been through the booklet. One caution if you do this – be sure to skip a number on your answer sheet as well. Check often to be sure that you have not lost your place and that you are marking in the row numbered the same as the question you are answering.

6) Read the questions

Be sure you know what the question asks! Many capable people are unsuccessful because they failed to *read* the questions correctly.

7) Answer all questions

Unless you have been instructed that a penalty will be deducted for incorrect answers, it is better to guess than to omit a question.

8) Speed tests

It is often better NOT to guess on speed tests. It has been found that on timed tests people are tempted to spend the last few seconds before time is called in marking answers at random – without even reading them – in the hope of picking up a few extra points. To discourage this practice, the instructions may warn you that your score will be "corrected" for guessing. That is, a penalty will be applied. The incorrect answers will be deducted from the correct ones, or some other penalty formula will be used.

9) Review your answers

If you finish before time is called, go back to the questions you guessed or omitted to give them further thought. Review other answers if you have time.

10) Return your test materials

If you are ready to leave before others have finished or time is called, take ALL your materials to the monitor and leave quietly. Never take any test material with you. The monitor can discover whose papers are not complete, and taking a test booklet may be grounds for disqualification.

VIII. EXAMINATION TECHNIQUES

1) Read the general instructions carefully. These are usually printed on the first page of the exam booklet. As a rule, these instructions refer to the timing of the examination; the fact that you should not start work until the signal and must stop work at a signal, etc. If there are any *special* instructions, such as a choice of questions to be answered, make sure that you note this instruction carefully.

2) When you are ready to start work on the examination, that is as soon as the signal has been given, read the instructions to each question booklet, underline any key words or phrases, such as *least, best, outline, describe* and the like. In this way you will tend to answer as requested rather than discover on reviewing your paper that you *listed without describing*, that you selected the *worst* choice rather than the *best* choice, etc.

3) If the examination is of the objective or multiple-choice type – that is, each question will also give a series of possible answers: A, B, C or D, and you are called upon to select the best answer and write the letter next to that answer on your answer paper – it is advisable to start answering each question in turn. There may be anywhere from 50 to 100 such questions in the three or four hours allotted and you can see how much time would be taken if you read through all the questions before beginning to answer any. Furthermore, if you come across a question or group of questions which you know would be difficult to answer, it would undoubtedly affect your handling of all the other questions.

4) If the examination is of the essay type and contains but a few questions, it is a moot point as to whether you should read all the questions before starting to answer any one. Of course, if you are given a choice – say five out of seven and the like – then it is essential to read all the questions so you can eliminate the two that are most difficult. If, however, you are asked to answer all the questions, there may be danger in trying to answer the easiest one first because you may find that you will spend too much time on it. The best technique is to answer the first question, then proceed to the second, etc.

5) Time your answers. Before the exam begins, write down the time it started, then add the time allowed for the examination and write down the time it must be completed, then divide the time available somewhat as follows:
   - If 3-1/2 hours are allowed, that would be 210 minutes. If you have 80 objective-type questions, that would be an average of 2-1/2 minutes per question. Allow yourself no more than 2 minutes per question, or a total of 160 minutes, which will permit about 50 minutes to review.
   - If for the time allotment of 210 minutes there are 7 essay questions to answer, that would average about 30 minutes a question. Give yourself only 25 minutes per question so that you have about 35 minutes to review.

6) The most important instruction is to *read each question* and make sure you know what is wanted. The second most important instruction is to *time yourself properly* so that you answer every question. The third most important instruction is to *answer every question*. Guess if you have to but include something for each question. Remember that you will receive no credit for a blank and will probably receive some credit if you write something in answer to an essay question. If you guess a letter – say "B" for a multiple-choice question – you may have guessed right. If you leave a blank as an answer to a multiple-choice question, the examiners may respect your feelings but it will not add a point to your score. Some exams may penalize you for wrong answers, so in such cases *only*, you may not want to guess unless you have some basis for your answer.

7) Suggestions
   a. Objective-type questions
      1. Examine the question booklet for proper sequence of pages and questions
      2. Read all instructions carefully
      3. Skip any question which seems too difficult; return to it after all other questions have been answered
      4. Apportion your time properly; do not spend too much time on any single question or group of questions

5. Note and underline key words – *all, most, fewest, least, best, worst, same, opposite,* etc.
6. Pay particular attention to negatives
7. Note unusual option, e.g., unduly long, short, complex, different or similar in content to the body of the question
8. Observe the use of "hedging" words – *probably, may, most likely,* etc.
9. Make sure that your answer is put next to the same number as the question
10. Do not second-guess unless you have good reason to believe the second answer is definitely more correct
11. Cross out original answer if you decide another answer is more accurate; do not erase until you are ready to hand your paper in
12. Answer all questions; guess unless instructed otherwise
13. Leave time for review

  b. Essay questions
1. Read each question carefully
2. Determine exactly what is wanted. Underline key words or phrases.
3. Decide on outline or paragraph answer
4. Include many different points and elements unless asked to develop any one or two points or elements
5. Show impartiality by giving pros and cons unless directed to select one side only
6. Make and write down any assumptions you find necessary to answer the questions
7. Watch your English, grammar, punctuation and choice of words
8. Time your answers; don't crowd material

8) Answering the essay question

Most essay questions can be answered by framing the specific response around several key words or ideas. Here are a few such key words or ideas:

M's: manpower, materials, methods, money, management
P's: purpose, program, policy, plan, procedure, practice, problems, pitfalls, personnel, public relations

  a. Six basic steps in handling problems:
1. Preliminary plan and background development
2. Collect information, data and facts
3. Analyze and interpret information, data and facts
4. Analyze and develop solutions as well as make recommendations
5. Prepare report and sell recommendations
6. Install recommendations and follow up effectiveness

  b. Pitfalls to avoid
1. *Taking things for granted* – A statement of the situation does not necessarily imply that each of the elements is necessarily true; for example, a complaint may be invalid and biased so that all that can be taken for granted is that a complaint has been registered

2. *Considering only one side of a situation* – Wherever possible, indicate several alternatives and then point out the reasons you selected the best one
3. *Failing to indicate follow up* – Whenever your answer indicates action on your part, make certain that you will take proper follow-up action to see how successful your recommendations, procedures or actions turn out to be
4. *Taking too long in answering any single question* – Remember to time your answers properly

IX. AFTER THE TEST

Scoring procedures differ in detail among civil service jurisdictions although the general principles are the same. Whether the papers are hand-scored or graded by machine we have described, they are nearly always graded by number. That is, the person who marks the paper knows only the number – never the name – of the applicant. Not until all the papers have been graded will they be matched with names. If other tests, such as training and experience or oral interview ratings have been given, scores will be combined. Different parts of the examination usually have different weights. For example, the written test might count 60 percent of the final grade, and a rating of training and experience 40 percent. In many jurisdictions, veterans will have a certain number of points added to their grades.

After the final grade has been determined, the names are placed in grade order and an eligible list is established. There are various methods for resolving ties between those who get the same final grade – probably the most common is to place first the name of the person whose application was received first. Job offers are made from the eligible list in the order the names appear on it. You will be notified of your grade and your rank as soon as all these computations have been made. This will be done as rapidly as possible.

People who are found to meet the requirements in the announcement are called "eligibles." Their names are put on a list of eligible candidates. An eligible's chances of getting a job depend on how high he stands on this list and how fast agencies are filling jobs from the list.

When a job is to be filled from a list of eligibles, the agency asks for the names of people on the list of eligibles for that job. When the civil service commission receives this request, it sends to the agency the names of the three people highest on this list. Or, if the job to be filled has specialized requirements, the office sends the agency the names of the top three persons who meet these requirements from the general list.

The appointing officer makes a choice from among the three people whose names were sent to him. If the selected person accepts the appointment, the names of the others are put back on the list to be considered for future openings.

That is the rule in hiring from all kinds of eligible lists, whether they are for typist, carpenter, chemist, or something else. For every vacancy, the appointing officer has his choice of any one of the top three eligibles on the list. This explains why the person whose name is on top of the list sometimes does not get an appointment when some of the persons lower on the list do. If the appointing officer chooses the second or third eligible, the No. 1 eligible does not get a job at once, but stays on the list until he is appointed or the list is terminated.

X. HOW TO PASS THE INTERVIEW TEST

The examination for which you applied requires an oral interview test. You have already taken the written test and you are now being called for the interview test – the final part of the formal examination.

You may think that it is not possible to prepare for an interview test and that there are no procedures to follow during an interview. Our purpose is to point out some things you can do in advance that will help you and some good rules to follow and pitfalls to avoid while you are being interviewed.

What is an interview supposed to test?

The written examination is designed to test the technical knowledge and competence of the candidate; the oral is designed to evaluate intangible qualities, not readily measured otherwise, and to establish a list showing the relative fitness of each candidate – as measured against his competitors – for the position sought. Scoring is not on the basis of "right" and "wrong," but on a sliding scale of values ranging from "not passable" to "outstanding." As a matter of fact, it is possible to achieve a relatively low score without a single "incorrect" answer because of evident weakness in the qualities being measured.

Occasionally, an examination may consist entirely of an oral test – either an individual or a group oral. In such cases, information is sought concerning the technical knowledges and abilities of the candidate, since there has been no written examination for this purpose. More commonly, however, an oral test is used to supplement a written examination.

Who conducts interviews?

The composition of oral boards varies among different jurisdictions. In nearly all, a representative of the personnel department serves as chairman. One of the members of the board may be a representative of the department in which the candidate would work. In some cases, "outside experts" are used, and, frequently, a businessman or some other representative of the general public is asked to serve. Labor and management or other special groups may be represented. The aim is to secure the services of experts in the appropriate field.

However the board is composed, it is a good idea (and not at all improper or unethical) to ascertain in advance of the interview who the members are and what groups they represent. When you are introduced to them, you will have some idea of their backgrounds and interests, and at least you will not stutter and stammer over their names.

What should be done before the interview?

While knowledge about the board members is useful and takes some of the surprise element out of the interview, there is other preparation which is more substantive. It *is* possible to prepare for an oral interview – in several ways:

1) Keep a copy of your application and review it carefully before the interview

This may be the only document before the oral board, and the starting point of the interview. Know what education and experience you have listed there, and the sequence and dates of all of it. Sometimes the board will ask you to review the highlights of your experience for them; you should not have to hem and haw doing it.

2) Study the class specification and the examination announcement

Usually, the oral board has one or both of these to guide them. The qualities, characteristics or knowledges required by the position sought are stated in these documents. They offer valuable clues as to the nature of the oral interview. For example, if the job involves supervisory responsibilities, the announcement will usually indicate that knowledge of modern supervisory methods and the qualifications of the candidate as a supervisor will be tested. If so, you can expect such questions, frequently in the form of a hypothetical situation which you are expected to solve. NEVER go into an oral without knowledge of the duties and responsibilities of the job you seek.

3) Think through each qualification required

Try to visualize the kind of questions you would ask if you were a board member. How well could you answer them? Try especially to appraise your own knowledge and background in each area, *measured against the job sought*, and identify any areas in which you are weak. Be critical and realistic – do not flatter yourself.

4) Do some general reading in areas in which you feel you may be weak

For example, if the job involves supervision and your past experience has NOT, some general reading in supervisory methods and practices, particularly in the field of human relations, might be useful. Do NOT study agency procedures or detailed manuals. The oral board will be testing your understanding and capacity, not your memory.

5) Get a good night's sleep and watch your general health and mental attitude

You will want a clear head at the interview. Take care of a cold or any other minor ailment, and of course, no hangovers.

What should be done on the day of the interview?

Now comes the day of the interview itself. Give yourself plenty of time to get there. Plan to arrive somewhat ahead of the scheduled time, particularly if your appointment is in the fore part of the day. If a previous candidate fails to appear, the board might be ready for you a bit early. By early afternoon an oral board is almost invariably behind schedule if there are many candidates, and you may have to wait. Take along a book or magazine to read, or your application to review, but leave any extraneous material in the waiting room when you go in for your interview. In any event, relax and compose yourself.

The matter of dress is important. The board is forming impressions about you – from your experience, your manners, your attitude, and your appearance. Give your personal appearance careful attention. Dress your best, but not your flashiest. Choose conservative, appropriate clothing, and be sure it is immaculate. This is a business interview, and your appearance should indicate that you regard it as such. Besides, being well groomed and properly dressed will help boost your confidence.

Sooner or later, someone will call your name and escort you into the interview room. *This is it.* From here on you are on your own. It is too late for any more preparation. But remember, you asked for this opportunity to prove your fitness, and you are here because your request was granted.

What happens when you go in?

The usual sequence of events will be as follows: The clerk (who is often the board stenographer) will introduce you to the chairman of the oral board, who will introduce you to the other members of the board. Acknowledge the introductions before you sit down. Do not be surprised if you find a microphone facing you or a stenotypist sitting by. Oral interviews are usually recorded in the event of an appeal or other review.

Usually the chairman of the board will open the interview by reviewing the highlights of your education and work experience from your application – primarily for the benefit of the other members of the board, as well as to get the material into the record. Do not interrupt or comment unless there is an error or significant misinterpretation; if that is the case, do not hesitate. But do not quibble about insignificant matters. Also, he will usually ask you some question about your education, experience or your present job – partly to get you to start talking and to establish the interviewing "rapport." He may start the actual questioning, or turn it over to one of the other members. Frequently, each member undertakes the questioning on a particular area, one in which he is perhaps most competent, so you can expect each member to participate in the examination. Because time is limited, you may also expect some rather abrupt switches in the direction the questioning takes, so do not be upset by it. Normally, a board member will not pursue a single line of questioning unless he discovers a particular strength or weakness.

After each member has participated, the chairman will usually ask whether any member has any further questions, then will ask you if you have anything you wish to add. Unless you are expecting this question, it may floor you. Worse, it may start you off on an extended, extemporaneous speech. The board is not usually seeking more information. The question is principally to offer you a last opportunity to present further qualifications or to indicate that you have nothing to add. So, if you feel that a significant qualification or characteristic has been overlooked, it is proper to point it out in a sentence or so. Do not compliment the board on the thoroughness of their examination – they have been sketchy, and you know it. If you wish, merely say, "No thank you, I have nothing further to add." This is a point where you can "talk yourself out" of a good impression or fail to present an important bit of information. Remember, *you close the interview yourself*.

The chairman will then say, "That is all, Mr. _____, thank you." Do not be startled; the interview is over, and quicker than you think. Thank him, gather your belongings and take your leave. Save your sigh of relief for the other side of the door.

How to put your best foot forward
Throughout this entire process, you may feel that the board individually and collectively is trying to pierce your defenses, seek out your hidden weaknesses and embarrass and confuse you. Actually, this is not true. They are obliged to make an appraisal of your qualifications for the job you are seeking, and they want to see you in your best light. Remember, they must interview all candidates and a non-cooperative candidate may become a failure in spite of their best efforts to bring out his qualifications. Here are 15 suggestions that will help you:

1) **Be natural – Keep your attitude confident, not cocky**
If you are not confident that you can do the job, do not expect the board to be. Do not apologize for your weaknesses, try to bring out your strong points. The board is interested in a positive, not negative, presentation. Cockiness will antagonize any board member and make him wonder if you are covering up a weakness by a false show of strength.

2) **Get comfortable, but don't lounge or sprawl**
Sit erectly but not stiffly. A careless posture may lead the board to conclude that you are careless in other things, or at least that you are not impressed by the importance of the occasion. Either conclusion is natural, even if incorrect. Do not fuss with your clothing, a pencil or an ashtray. Your hands may occasionally be useful to emphasize a point; do not let them become a point of distraction.

3) **Do not wisecrack or make small talk**
This is a serious situation, and your attitude should show that you consider it as such. Further, the time of the board is limited – they do not want to waste it, and neither should you.

4) Do not exaggerate your experience or abilities

In the first place, from information in the application or other interviews and sources, the board may know more about you than you think. Secondly, you probably will not get away with it. An experienced board is rather adept at spotting such a situation, so do not take the chance.

5) If you know a board member, do not make a point of it, yet do not hide it

Certainly you are not fooling him, and probably not the other members of the board. Do not try to take advantage of your acquaintanceship – it will probably do you little good.

6) Do not dominate the interview

Let the board do that. They will give you the clues – do not assume that you have to do all the talking. Realize that the board has a number of questions to ask you, and do not try to take up all the interview time by showing off your extensive knowledge of the answer to the first one.

7) Be attentive

You only have 20 minutes or so, and you should keep your attention at its sharpest throughout. When a member is addressing a problem or question to you, give him your undivided attention. Address your reply principally to him, but do not exclude the other board members.

8) Do not interrupt

A board member may be stating a problem for you to analyze. He will ask you a question when the time comes. Let him state the problem, and wait for the question.

9) Make sure you understand the question

Do not try to answer until you are sure what the question is. If it is not clear, restate it in your own words or ask the board member to clarify it for you. However, do not haggle about minor elements.

10) Reply promptly but not hastily

A common entry on oral board rating sheets is "candidate responded readily," or "candidate hesitated in replies." Respond as promptly and quickly as you can, but do not jump to a hasty, ill-considered answer.

11) Do not be peremptory in your answers

A brief answer is proper – but do not fire your answer back. That is a losing game from your point of view. The board member can probably ask questions much faster than you can answer them.

12) Do not try to create the answer you think the board member wants

He is interested in what kind of mind you have and how it works – not in playing games. Furthermore, he can usually spot this practice and will actually grade you down on it.

13) Do not switch sides in your reply merely to agree with a board member

Frequently, a member will take a contrary position merely to draw you out and to see if you are willing and able to defend your point of view. Do not start a debate, yet do not surrender a good position. If a position is worth taking, it is worth defending.

14) Do not be afraid to admit an error in judgment if you are shown to be wrong

The board knows that you are forced to reply without any opportunity for careful consideration. Your answer may be demonstrably wrong. If so, admit it and get on with the interview.

15) Do not dwell at length on your present job

The opening question may relate to your present assignment. Answer the question but do not go into an extended discussion. You are being examined for a *new* job, not your present one. As a matter of fact, try to phrase ALL your answers in terms of the job for which you are being examined.

Basis of Rating

Probably you will forget most of these "do's" and "don'ts" when you walk into the oral interview room. Even remembering them all will not ensure you a passing grade. Perhaps you did not have the qualifications in the first place. But remembering them will help you to put your best foot forward, without treading on the toes of the board members.

Rumor and popular opinion to the contrary notwithstanding, an oral board wants you to make the best appearance possible. They know you are under pressure – but they also want to see how you respond to it as a guide to what your reaction would be under the pressures of the job you seek. They will be influenced by the degree of poise you display, the personal traits you show and the manner in which you respond.

ABOUT THIS BOOK

This book contains tests divided into Examination Sections. Go through each test, answering every question in the margin. We have also attached a sample answer sheet at the back of the book that can be removed and used. At the end of each test look at the answer key and check your answers. On the ones you got wrong, look at the right answer choice and learn. Do not fill in the answers first. Do not memorize the questions and answers, but understand the answer and principles involved. On your test, the questions will likely be different from the samples. Questions are changed and new ones added. If you understand these past questions you should have success with any changes that arise. Tests may consist of several types of questions. We have additional books on each subject should more study be advisable or necessary for you. Finally, the more you study, the better prepared you will be. This book is intended to be the last thing you study before you walk into the examination room. Prior study of relevant texts is also recommended. NLC publishes some of these in our Fundamental Series. Knowledge and good sense are important factors in passing your exam. Good luck also helps. So now study this Passbook, absorb the material contained within and take that knowledge into the examination. Then do your best to pass that exam.

EXAMINATION SECTION

EXAMINATION SECTION
TEST 1

DIRECTIONS: Each question or incomplete statement is followed by several suggested answers or completions. Select the one that BEST answers the question or completes the statement. *PRINT THE LETTER OF THE CORRECT ANSWER IN THE SPACE AT THE RIGHT.*

1. The one of the following devices that is required on BOTH coal-fired and oil-fired boilers is a(n)
    A. safety valve
    B. low water cut-off
    C. feedwater regulator
    D. electrostatic precipitator

    1.____

2. Lowering the thermostat setting by 5 degrees during the heating season will result in a fuel saving of MOST NEARLY _____ percent.
    A. 2   B. 5   C. 20   D. 50

    2.____

3. An electrically-driven rotary fuel oil pump must be protected from internal damage by the installation in the oil line of a
    A. discharge-side strainer
    B. check valve
    C. suction gauge
    D. pressure relief valve

    3.____

4. A float-thermostatic steam trap in a condensate return line that is operating properly will allow _____ to pass and will hold back _____.
    A. steam and air; condensate
    B. air and condensate; steam
    C. steam and condensate; air
    D. steam; air and condensate

    4.____

5. Changes in the combustion efficiency of a boiler can be determined by comparing changes in stack temperature and
    A. steam pressure in the header
    B. over-the-fire draft
    C. percentage of carbon dioxide
    D. equivalent direct radiation

    5.____

6. The classification of the coal that is USUALLY burned in school buildings is
    A. anthracite
    B. bituminous
    C. semi-bituminous
    D. lignite

    6.____

7. A boiler is equipped with the following pressurtrols:
    I. Manual-reset pressurtrol
    II. Modulating pressurtrol
    III. High-limit pressurtrol
    The CORRECT sequence in which these devices should be actuated by rising steam pressure is:
    A. I, II, III   B. II, III, I   C. III, I, II   D. III, II, I

    7.____

    8.____

8. The temperature of the returning condensate in a low-pressure steam heating system is 195°F.
   This temperature indicates that
   A. some radiator traps are defective
   B. some boiler tubes are leaking
   C. the boiler water level is too low
   D. there is a high vacuum in the return line

9. An over-the-fire draft gauge in a natural draft furnace is USUALLY read in
   A. feet per minute   B. pounds per square inch
   C. inches of mercury   D. inches of water

10. The equipment which is used to provide tempered fresh air to certain areas of a school building is a(n)
    A. exhaust fan   B. window fan   C. fixed louvre   D. heating stack

11. A chemical FREQUENTLY used to melt ice on outdoor pavement is
    A. ammonia   B. soda
    C. carbon tetrachloride D. calcium chloride

12. A herbicide is a chemical PRIMARILY used as a(n)
    A. disinfectant   B. fertilizer   C. insect killer   D. weed killer

13. Established plants that continue to blossom year after year without reseeding are GENERALLY known as
    A. annuals   B. parasites   C. perennials   D. symbiotics

14. A ferrous sulfate solution is sometimes used to treat shrubs or trees that have a deficiency of
    A. boron   B. copper   C. iron   D. zinc

15. A tree is described as deciduous.
    This means PRIMARILY that it
    A. bears nuts instead of fruit   B. has been pruned recently
    C. usually grows in swampy ground   D. loses its leaves in the fall

16. If you are told that a container holds a 20-7-7 fertilizer, it is MOST likely that twenty percent of this fertilizer is
    A. nitrogen   B. oxygen
    C. phosphoric acid   D. potash

17. The landscape drawings for a school indicate the planting of *Acer platanoides* at a certain location on the grounds.
    Acer platanoides is a type of
    A. privet hedge   B. rose bush   C. maple tree   D. tulip bed

18. A cleaner is attempting to lift a heavy drum of liquid cleaner from the floor to a shelf at waist height.
    He is MOST likely to avoid personal injury in lifting the drum if he
    A. keeps his back as straight as possible and lifts the weight primarily with his back muscles
    B. arches his back and lifts the weight primarily with his back muscles
    C. keeps his back as straight as possible and lifts the weight primarily with his leg muscles
    D. arches his back and lifts the weight primarily with his leg muscles

18.____

19. Of the following, the BEST first aid treatment for a cleaner who has burned his hand with dry caustic lye crystals is to
    A. wash his hand with large quantities of warm water
    B. brush his hand lightly with a soft, clean brush and wrap it in a clean rag
    C. place his hand in a mild solution of ammonia and cool water
    D. wash his hand with large quantities of cold water

19.____

20. The purpose of the third prong in a three-prong electric plug used on a 120-volt electric vacuum cleaner is to prevent
    A. serious overheating of the vacuum cleaner
    B. electric shock to the operator of the vacuum cleaner
    C. generation of dangerous microwaves by the vacuum cleaner
    D. sparking in the electric outlet caused by a loose electric plug

20.____

21. Of the following, the LEAST effective method for a school custodian to use to reduce window glass breakage in his school is to
    A. keep the area near the school free of sticks and stones
    B. consult with parents and civic organizations and request their assistance in reducing breakage
    C. request that neighbors living near the school report after-hours incidents to the police department
    D. develop a reputation as a *tough guy* with the students so that they will be afraid to break windows in the school

21.____

22. The one of the following procedures that a school custodian should use when a telephone caller makes a threat to place a bomb in the school building is to
    A. hang up on the caller
    B. keep the caller talking as long as possible and make notes on what he says
    C. tell the caller he has the wrong number
    D. tell the caller his voice is being recorded and the call is being traced to its source

22.____

23. A school custodian is responsible for enforcing certain safety regulations in the school.
    The MOST important reason for enforcing safety regulations is that
    A. every accident can be prevented
    B. compliance with safety regulations will make all other safety efforts unnecessary

23.____

C. safety regulations are the law, and law enforcement is an end in itself
D. safety regulations are based on reason and experience with the best methods of accident prevention

24. The safety belts that are worn by cleaners when washing outside windows should be inspected
    A. before each use
    B. weekly
    C. monthly
    D. semi-annually

24._____

25. The one of the following actions that a school custodian should take to help reduce burglary losses in the school is to
    A. leave all the lights on in the school overnight
    B. see that interior and exterior doors are securely locked at the end of the day
    C. set booby traps that will severely injure anyone breaking in
    D. set up an apartment in the school basement and stay at the school every night

25._____

KEY (CORRECT ANSWERS)

1.	A	11.	D
2.	C	12.	D
3.	D	13.	C
4.	B	14.	C
5.	C	15.	D
6.	A	16.	A
7.	B	17.	C
8.	A	18.	C
9.	D	19.	D
10.	D	20.	B

21.	D
22.	B
23.	D
24.	A
25.	B

EXAMINATION SECTION
TEST 1

DIRECTIONS: Each question or incomplete statement is followed by several suggested answers or completions. Select the one that BEST answers the question or completes the statement. *PRINT THE LETTER OF THE CORRECT ANSWER IN THE SPACE AT THE RIGHT.*

1. Roaches are LEAST likely to be found in 1.____
    A. toilet rooms
    B. locker rooms
    C. offices
    D. waste paper rooms

2. A star drill is used to 2.____
    A. cut an old nipple from a fitting
    B. groove metal
    C. drill holes in stone and brick
    D. drill star-shaped holes in hard wood

3. A flushometer is a device which 3.____
    A. measures the velocity of flow of water through a toilet fixture
    B. acts as a valve in low tanks on water closet
    C. acts as a valve in high tanks on water closet
    D. releases water to flush water closets of the tankless type

4. The type of valve which LEAST obstructs the flow of water in water lines is the _____ valve. 4.____
    A. gate
    B. pressure regulating
    C. angle
    D. globe

5. The purpose of a sump pump is to 5.____
    A. lift cellar drainage into a sewer
    B. clear a stoppage in a toilet fixture
    C. empty radiators of water condensate
    D. keep water pressure in boilers constant

6. A bibb reseater is used in the repair of 6.____
    A. faucets
    B. gate valves
    C. scaly fusible plugs
    D. check valves

7. A *plumber's friend* is a device used to clear a stoppage in a 7.____
    A. drainage line
    B. vent line
    C. house sewer
    D. water supply fixture

8. Which of the following statements about tools and their uses in INCORRECT? 8.____
    A. A wrench should never be used as a hammer.
    B. A screwdriver should not be used as a chisel.
    C. When removing a bit from a hole after boring, turn the bit all the way.
    D. Before using a chisel, make sure that the head is mushroomed.

Questions 9-12.

DIRECTIONS: Column I lists tools used by a custodian. The uses of tools are given in Column II. Select the CORRECT use for the tools listed and place the letter representing your choice next to the number of the tool in the space at the right.

	COLUMN I		COLUMN II	
9.	Center punch	A.	Punch round holes in center of metal sheets	9.___
		B.	Turn headless set screw	
10.	Cold chisel	C.	Mark location of a hole to be drilled	10.___
		D.	Cut wood parallel or with the grain	
11.	Rip saw	E.	Cut across the grain of wood	11.___
		F.	Cut off a rivet head	
12.	Allen wrench	G.	Turn flat-head wood screws	12.___

13. Too hold a piece of lumber in place, the length of nail should be _____ the thickness of the lumber.   13.___
    A. three times   B. equal to
    C. one and one-half times   D. half

14.   14.___

METER READING AT BEGINNING OF PERIOD

METER READING AT END OF PERIOD

The above are the readings on the electric meter at the beginning and end of a period.
The TOTAL kilowatt hour consumption is
    A. 264   B. 570   C. 61   D. 175

15. Proper combustion of fuel is obtained when   15.___
    A. the flue gases contain a large percentage of carbon monoxide
    B. black smoke appears in the flue gases
    C. there is 10 to 15 percent carbon dioxide in the flue gases
    D. the flame of the fire is high enough to reach the fire tubes

16. The vertical pipes leading from the steam mains to the radiators are called 16.____
    A. expansion joints B. radiant coils
    C. drip lines D. risers

17. Try cocks are used to 17.____
    A. determine the exact water level in the boiler
    B. find the approximate water level in the boiler
    C. learn if steam is being generated in the boiler
    D. obtain an approximate idea of the steam pressure

18. If a ton of anthracite coal occupies approximately 40 cubic feet, the space required, in cubic yards, for 135 tons of coal is 18.____
    A. 200 B. 128.6 C. 600 D. 40

19. During the winter heating season, it is BEST practice to blow down the boiler 19.____
    A. once a month
    B. twice daily
    C. only when new grates are installed
    D. once a day

20. A boiler blow-off valve is PRIMARILY used to 20.____
    A. maintain constant boiler pressure
    B. drain water from boiler
    C. allow air to enter boiler when proper temperature is reached
    D. reduce boiler pressure

21. When a room becomes heated above the upper temperature setting of a thermostat which controls a check damper, the damper is 21.____
    A. automatically closed to reduce the air supply
    B. opened to admit more air
    C. not affected, but the supply of the boiler is increased
    D. partially closed and the water supply of the boiler is increased

22. When a custodian finds that the water level of his boiler is dangerously low, he should 22.____
    A. open his drafts
    B. immediately fill boiler with cold water
    C. cover the fire with wet ashes
    D. close all air openings to the fire box

23. Which one of the following is NOT a good method in banking fires? 23.____
    A. A little ash should be left on that portion of the fire not banked.
    B. The coal should be covered with ashes to preserve the fire.
    C. The dampers should be closed except for a small opening to admit a little air.
    D. Ashes should be removed from the ashpit.

24. Radiators radiate more heat when they are painted with
    A. bronze paint
    B. aluminum paint
    C. regular wall paint
    D. shellac

25. When a boiler is laid up for the summer, one of the things NOT to do is
    A. tap brace and stary rods with a hammer to detect loose ends
    B. leave water in boiler if basement is damp
    C. close all hand holes and manholes to prevent dust and air from getting into the cleaned boiler
    D. clean gauge glasses with muriatic acid to dissolve the accumulations of lime and other deposits

---

KEY (CORRECT ANSWERS)

1.	C	11.	D
2.	C	12.	B
3.	D	13.	A
4.	A	14.	D
5.	A	15.	C
6.	A	16.	D
7.	A	17.	B
8.	D	18.	A
9.	C	19.	D
10.	F	20.	B

21.	B
22.	C
23.	B
24.	B
25.	C

TEST 2

DIRECTIONS: Each question or incomplete statement is followed by several suggested answers or completions. Select the one that BEST answers the question or completes the statement. *PRINT THE LETTER OF THE CORRECT ANSWER IN THE SPACE AT THE RIGHT.*

1. A heating plant is to be laid up for the summer. 1.____
   With respect to fire surfaces, the PROPER procedure after cleaning is to
   A. keep them moist with water applied with a spray
   B. paint them with a good plastic paint
   C. coat them with oil
   D. paint them with a metallic paint

2. When starting a fire in the boiler, the custodian should 2.____
   A. have asphalt doors and dampers closed before firing to give proper draft
   B. place about one inch of coal directly on the grate and then ignite with oil waste
   C. keep dampers closed and ashpit doors open to obtain proper drafts
   D. spread a bed of coal about three inches thick on the grates and then build fire on this bed

3. The vacuum system of storm heating does NOT have 3.____
   A. air valves on radiators
   B. thermostatic traps on radiators
   C. drip traps
   D. steam risers connected to radiators

4. The capacity of a heating boiler is USUALLY expressed in terms of 4.____
   A. square feet of radiation   B. cubic feet of steam
   C. pounds of steam per hour   D. the number of radiators required

5. The hammering noise in a heating system is caused by 5.____
   A. the pressure of water acting against the walls of the water pipe supplying the boiler
   B. contact of steam and water in the radiators
   C. the vibration of loose fire tubes in the boiler
   D. the vacuum effect of the release of water in the steam gauge

6. In one hour, one square foot of grate for a tubular boiler will burn, with 6.____
   natural draft, about _____ lbs. of hard coal.
   A. 12   B. 25   C. 6   D. 30

7. When priming occurs in a boiler, 7.____
   A. the fire will be extinguished
   B. the steam becomes superheated and too dry
   C. the fire tubes become overheated and may crack
   D. water particles are carried over with the steam into the steam lines

9

8. One of the ways to prevent or reduce the amount of smoke from a furnace is to
   A. reduce the quantity of air supplied to the fire box
   B. supply coal in large quantities and no more than twice a day
   C. cool the fire bed to prevent high temperatures in the fire box
   D. keep live coals at the top of the fire bed

9. Of the following, the SMALLEST size coal is
   A. chestnut   B. egg   C. buckwheat   D. pea

10. If coal is to be stored, the following precaution should be followed:
    A. Coal should be piled in conical piles rather than horizontal layers
    B. Coal should be placed in storage on hot summer days
    C. Avoid alternate wetting and drying of coal
    D. Coal should be piled no more than three feet deep

11. The HRT boiler contains
    A. fire tubes in which hot gases flow
    B. water tubes in which water flows to form steam
    C. no horizontal return tubes
    D. no way in which a vacuum return can be connected

12. A classroom is properly heated in the winter time when the temperature is about _____°F and the relative humidity is _____%.
    A. 70; 40 to 60   B. 78; 40 to 60   C. 65; 30   D. 75; 90

13. The average temperature on a day in January 30°F. This would be called a _____ degree day.
    A. 40   B. 35   C. 30   D. 25

14. The term BTU is used in connection with
    A. heating quality or a fuel   B. the size of boiler tubes
    C. radiator fittings   D. heating qualities of radiators

15. Which one of the following is NOT the cause of clinker formation?
    A. Poor quality coal
    B. Thick fires
    C. Closed ashpit doors
    D. Water sprayed into the ashpit at intervals during the day

16. When a spot has burned through the fire bed, it is a GOOD plan to
    A. fill the burned out hole with green coal
    B. push burning coals to that part of the grate before spreading green coal on it
    C. fill that part of the grate with cold ashes, then place green coal on it
    D. fill the spot with excelsior and then place green coal on it

17. Thin spots or holes in a fire bed are USUALLY
    A. developed in the front part or center of the fire bed
    B. developed near the back or corners of the fire bed
    C. located where there is a smoky, dull flame
    D. the result of burning soft coal

18. With respect to the operation of univents, the custodian should
    A. close the steam valve supplying the unit radiators at the close of school every day
    B. see that the steam valve supplying the unit radiators is never closed except when repairs are required
    C. shut off the univents at the close of the day by pulling the main switch
    D. make certain that no part of the uninvent has water in it

19. Ventilating systems for toilets usually should be separate from the building ventilating system because
    A. it prevents toilet odors from reaching rooms
    B. toilets need a more dependable ventilating system
    C. the requirements of the two systems are different
    D. only the toilets need ventilating in summer

20. When the flues of a boiler require frequent cleaning, the PROBABLE cause is
    A. excess draft
    B. too high a rate of combustion
    C. incomplete combustion
    D. lack of clinker formation

21. Generally, the part of the building where the highest temperature is maintained in the wintertime is the
    A. corridors
    B. toilets
    C. gymnasium
    D. regular classrooms

22. A template is a
    A. round disc used to close openings in walls where a fixture has been removed
    B. pattern that has been cut, bent, or molded to a definite shape and size
    C. plate used under machines or motors to catch excess oil
    D. metal form to be placed behind radiators to protect the wall

23. A student slips on the floor of the entrance to the school building. A lawyer representing the family of the child asks for information concerning the accident.
    The custodian should
    A. be cooperative and give all details concerning the accident and the condition of the entrance
    B. tell the lawyer that he will give the desired information if the child's parents give their consent
    C. refer the lawyer to the legal division of the Board of Education for information concerning the matter
    D. refuse to allow the lawyer to enter the school building

24. A teacher tells you that waxing a rubber tile floor is dangerous because the floor becomes too slippery.
    Your response should be
    A. that the children should be careful in walking on these floors and should wear rubber heels to avoid slipping
    B. an explanation of the non-slippery properties of a water emulsion wax properly applied
    C. tell her to mind her own business
    D. that it is not dangerous because no children have fallen and injured themselves

25. To order wet mop filler replacements, a custodian should specify the
    A. number of strands
    B. girth
    C. weight
    D. wet test strength

KEY (CORRECT ANSWERS)

1.	C		11.	A
2.	D		12.	A
3.	A		13.	B
4.	A		14.	A
5.	B		15.	D
6.	A		16.	B
7.	D		17.	B
8.	D		18.	B
9.	C		19.	C
10.	C		20.	C

21. D
22. B
23. C
24. B
25. C

EXAMINATION SECTION
TEST 1

DIRECTIONS: Each question or incomplete statement is followed by several suggested answers or completions. Select the one that BEST answers the question or completes the statement. *PRINT THE LETTER OF THE CORRECT ANSWER IN THE SPACE AT THE RIGHT.*

1. The safety device on an elevator door is called the 1.____
   A. governor   B. gate-switch   C. interlock   D. safety fuse

2. Which of the following is the PROPER method of cleaning a room? 2.____
   A. Dust, empty wastebasket, sweep
   B. Empty wastebasket, dust, sweep
   C. Empty wastebasket, sweep, dust
   D. Sweep, dust, empty wastebasket

3. How would you determine when a waxed floor should be stripped? 3.____
   When
   A. someone slipped on the floor
   B. wax builds up
   C. scuffs are not removed by buffing
   D. someone complains

4. To remove modeling plaster from the floor, you should use 4.____
   A. a sharp chisel   B. a putty knife
   C. a floor-scrubbing machine D. sulphuric acid

5. Which of the following floors would you NOT seal? 5.____
   A. Terrazzo   B. Cork   C. Asphalt   D. Tile

6. A mixing valve for domestic water blends 6.____
   A. cold water with hot boiler water
   B. hot and cold water
   C. cold water and hot water from coil submerged in boiler water
   D. hot and cold water from cooling coil

7. For sweeping under the radiators, the BEST tool to use is a 7.____
   A. dry mop   B. feather duster
   C. counter brush   D. floor broom

8. A wet return line is 8.____
   A. one containing air and water   B. above boiler water level
   C. below boiler water level   D. a condenser oil

9. A dry return line is
   A. one containing air only
   B. above boiler water level
   C. one containing air and water
   D. a line with a bleeder valve

10. The purpose of a fusetron is to
    A. provide motor starting current
    B. keep motor at rated speed
    C. protect from overload
    D. maintain constant motor speed

11. If combination faucet is in off position and water leaks from swivel, you should
    A. replace faucet washers
    B. repack swivel gland
    C. replace both washers and tighten swivel gland
    D. replace the faucet

12. The MAIN purpose of peat moss use is to
    A. improve soil condition
    B. fertilize soil
    C. help to keep soil moist
    D. retard the growth of weeds

13. Which of the following valves does NOT have a wheel and stem?
    A. Globe
    B. Gate
    C. Check
    D. Plug cock

14. If a radiator is air-bound, the MOST likely cause is
    A. no condensate return
    B. defective steam valve
    C. defective air valve
    D. too much air carried in steam

15. The MAIN purpose of keeping accident reports on file is to
    A. have a record to show a lawyer
    B. contain cause of accident
    C. inform principal of how it happened
    D. provide full information for official use

16. To repair a continually flushing flushometer, you should
    A. cut down on supply valve
    B. shut off water
    C. clean out flushometer
    D. replace defective parts

17. When a repair is required, the LEAST likely thing to be done is:
    A. Determine if your staff can handle it
    B. Find out just what has to be done
    C. Ask for assistance from repair shops
    D. Decide which tools are needed to do the job

18. At which of the following locations should you find a remote control switch?
    A. In principal's office
    B. In engineer's office
    C. At boiler room entrance
    D. At entrance to building

19. Sprinkler systems are more often found in the following location:
    A. Boiler room
    B. Gym
    C. Storage rooms
    D. Science rooms

20. If a gas range flame is all whitish yellow, what does it indicate?
    A. Insufficient gas pressure B. Insufficient air
    C. Not enough gas D. Too much air

21. If glass on water column breaks when boiler is operating, you should
    A. bank fire B. shut off burner
    C. use tri-cocks D. close main steam valve

22. The BEST reason for setting a time limit on the job is
    A. time available
    B. if completion is urgent
    C. if maximum output is affected this way
    D. the men are more likely to complete the job on time

23. The safety device on a gas line is called
    A. gas cock B. automatic pilot
    C. solenoid valve D. safety shut-off valve

24. The MOST efficient boiler fuel operation is
    A. low CO_2 high CO, low stack gas temperature
    B. high CO_2 low CO, low stack gas temperature
    C. high firebox temperature, high CO_2 high stack temperature
    D. high CO_2 low CO, high stack gas temperature

25. The central vacuum cleaning system should be cleaned
    A. weekly B. twice weekly
    C. daily D. when necessary

26. If you had too much oil, what would you do for good combustion?
    A. Increase secondary air B. Increase primary air
    C. Increase both D. Lower oil pressure

27. The purpose of blowing down the water column is to
    A. make sure there is enough water
    B. keep the gauge glass clean
    C. determine the true water level
    D. make sure you have steam in boiler

28. Water hammer in water lines is caused by
    A. velocity of air and water
    B. defective faucet
    C. defective washers
    D. quick opening and closing of faucets

29. The CHIEF reason for a plumbing system trap is to
    A. equalize waste B. provide good drainage
    C. provide water seal D. none of the above

30. A vapor barrier is used for
    A. insulating electrically
    B. protecting against low temperature
    C. a moisture barrier
    D. exterior condensation on cold water pipes

31. The material recommended for removing blood or fruit stains from concrete is
    A. soft soap   B. neatsfoot oil   C. oxalic acid   D. ammonia

32. For what purpose are panic bars used? To
    A. make sure door is locked   B. provide easy exit
    C. meet fire department regulations   D. keep door open

33. To detect a leak in the gas line, which of the following would you do?
    A. Call gas company   B. Use a soapy solution
    C. Use a lighted match   D. Smell the area

34. To preserve freshly laid concrete, you would
    A. cover it   B. keep it moist
    C. keep it at a temperature of 60°F   C. keep it at a temperature over 60°F

35. Gas is measured in
    A. thousands cubic feet   B. hundreds cubic feet
    C. ten thousands cubic feet volume D. 100,000 cubic feet volume

36. The FIRST thing a window cleaner should do is
    A. test window bolts   B. see that cleaning tools are good
    C. check window belt   D. not lean too heavily on glass

37. Couplings on gas supply line serve the same purpose as
    A. electrical conduit   B. machine threads
    C. right and left hand   D. water unions

38. Before a custodian leaves the building, he would be LEAST likely to
    A. lower the flag   B. remove hazards
    C. tidy the stock room   D. check all entry doors

39. Which of the following would you NOT use to paint chain-link fences?
    A. Brush   B. Sprayer
    C. Roller   D. None of the above

40. Which of the following steps should be taken in closing a low pressure boiler at the end of heating season in preparation for lay-up?
    A. Empty water, close valves, drop fire
    B. Dump fire, close valves, let boiler cool, empty water
    C. Dump fire, let boiler cool, empty water, close valves
    D. None of the above

KEY (CORRECT ANSWERS)

1.	C	11.	A	21.	C	31.	D
2.	C	12.	C	22.	D	32.	B
3.	B	13.	C	23.	C	33.	B
4.	B	14.	C	24.	B	34.	B
5.	C	15.	D	25.	B	35.	A
6.	B	16.	D	26.	B	36.	C
7.	C	17.	C	27.	C	37.	C
8.	C	18.	C	28.	A	38.	C
9.	B	19.	C	29.	C	39.	B
10.	C	20.	D	30.	C	40.	B

TEST 2

DIRECTIONS: Each question or incomplete statement is followed by several suggested answers or completions. Select the one that BEST answers the question or completes the statement. *PRINT THE LETTER OF THE CORRECT ANSWER IN THE SPACE AT THE RIGHT.*

1. The lowest visible part of the water column attached to an HRT boiler should be AT LEAST
    A. 3 inches above the top row of tubes
    B. 6 inches above the fusible plug
    C. 1 inch above the top row of tubes
    D. ½ inch above the fusible plug

1.____

2. The function of a fusible plug is to
    A. melt if the water temperature is too high
    B. prevent too high a furnace temperature
    C. prevent excessive steam pressure from developing in the boiler
    D. melt when the water level drops below the level of the plug

2.____

3. To control the temperature of water in a domestic water supply tank, the device used is USUALLY a
    A. thermostat
    B. pressuretrol
    C. solenoid valve
    D. aquastat

3.____

4. A house trap is a device placed in the house drain immediately inside the foundation wall of the building.
   Its MAIN purpose is to
    A. trap sediment flowing in the house drain to the street sewer
    B. prevent sewer gases from circulating in the building plumbing system
    C. maintain air pressure balance in the vent lines of the plumbing system
    D. provide a means for cleaning the waste lines of the plumbing system

4.____

5. In the care and operation of steam boilers, a procedure that is considered GOOD practice is to
    A. open the safety valve in the event low water is found
    B. refill the boiler with cold water when the boiler is hot
    C. remove the boiler from service immediately if the water level cannot be determined because the gauge glass is broken
    D. use hot water where possible in refilling a boiler prior to firing

5.____

6. The addition of moisture to coal to promote combustion of coal is commonly referred to as
    A. tempering   B. dusting   C. watering   D. dehumidifying

6.____

7. The purpose of fire doors in a building is to
    A. prevent fires
    B. prevent arson
    C. avoid panic
    D. prevent the spread of fire

7.____

8. Of the following, the type of fire extinguisher that is MOST satisfactory for use on a fire in a place of operating electrical equipment is
   A. carbon dioxide
   B. sand pail
   C. soda acid
   D. foam

9. The device which is LEAST likely to be used by the custodian in cleaning minor stoppages in the plumbing system is a
   A. snake   B. auger   C. plunger   D. trowel

10. The PROPER cleaning agent for a paint brush that has been used to shellac a floor is
    A. gasoline   B. linseed oil   C. alcohol   D. turpentine

11. In cutting the ends of a number of lengths of wood at an angle of 45°, one would PREFERABLY use a
    A. protractor
    B. triangle
    C. miter box
    D. movable head T-square

12. To the custodian, the term *zeolite* refers to
    A. boiler insulation
    B. combustion chamber refractories
    C. boiler tube cleaning agent
    D. boiler water softening

13. A custodian notices a man in a corridor of the building. This visitor identifies himself as a police officer and states that he is observing a student in one of the classes.
    The custodian
    A. make no further inquiry of the police officer
    B. ask the police officer to check with the school principal if he has not already done so
    C. ask for all details, the name of the student, and reason for observation so that he can report the visit in his log book
    D. ask the police officer to leave the building unless he has received permission from the Board of Education in writing

14. When a paint coat blisters, the cause is USUALLY:
    A. Paint coat is too thick
    B. Plaster pores not sealed properly
    C. Moisture under the paint coat
    D. Too much oil in paint

15. Galvanized iron pails resist rusting because the surface of the iron is coated with
    A. copper   B. zinc   C. aluminum   D. lead

16. To maintain brick walls and to eliminate or prevent leaks, the walls are USUALLY
    A. painted   B. sprayed   C. pointed   D. refaced

17. A safety device that can be used instead of a fuse to protect a piece of electrical equipment is a
    A. circuit breaker
    B. rheostat
    C. toggle switch
    D. relay

    17.____

18. Custodians are required to abide by snow removal regulations, which state that snow be removed
    A. from sidewalks within four hours after snow ceases to fall during daytime
    B. from sidewalks within 24 hours after snowfall ceases
    C. within a reasonable period only from walks immediately in front of school entrances
    D. from sidewalks within 12 hours only if the fall is greater than four inches

    18.____

19. Which of the following types of grates should be used for ease in cleaning fires when hand firing large boilers under natural draft at heavy loads with #1 buckwheat?
    A. Dumping grates
    B. Stationary grates with ¾" air spaces
    C. Stationary grates (pinhole type)
    D. Shaking grates

    19.____

20. Which of the following fuels contains the GREATEST number of heat units per pound?
    A. Hard coal
    B. #6 fuel oil
    C. Yard screenings
    D. Bituminous coal

    20.____

21. The purpose of admitting air over the fire in a coal-fired furnace is USUALLY to
    A. reduce the stack gases temperature
    B. improve the draft
    C. reduce the smoke
    D. reduce the draft

    21.____

22. In most usual types of large capacity oil burners using #6 oil, under fully automatic control, the atomization of the oil is produced by the
    A. pressure from the pump
    B. pressure from the secondary air fan
    C. oil temperature from the heater
    D. rotation of the burner assembly by the motor

    2.____

23. Which of the following comes the closest to indicating the number of degree-days in a normal heating season in New York City?
    A. 3000
    B. 4000
    C. 5000
    D. 6000

    3.____

24. A badly sooted HRT boiler under coal firing will show a ____ than a clean boiler.
    A. higher CO_2 value
    B. lower CO_2 value
    C. higher stack temperature
    D. lower draft loss

    24.____

25. The direct room radiator in a school with a pneumatically controlled steam heating system is cold, while the adjoining rooms are heated adequately.
Of the following, the FIRST thing you would check in the room is the
    A. steam pipe in the room before the pneumatic steam valve
    B. thermostat
    C. pneumatic steam valve
    D. thermostatic trap

26. A vaporstat used on a fully automatic heavy oil burning rotary cup installation, with separate motor driven oil pump, is GENERALLY used to
    A. keep the boiler pressure within proper limits
    B. regulate the pressure of the primary air
    C. regulate the pressure of the secondary air
    D. shut down the burner when primary air failure occurs

27. Suppose that a small oil fire has broken out in the boiler room of your building.
Of the following, the one that is LEAST suitable as an extinguisher is
    A. soda acid
    B. pyrene (carbon tetra chloride
    C. foamite
    D. carbon dioxide

28. An electric elevator car stalls on the ground floor of a school building.
Of the following, the item you would be LEAST likely to check in your inspection is
    A. *baby switch*
    B. floor door switch
    C. limit switch
    D. current to elevator motors

29. In an investigation of a complaint of sewer gas from a urinal in a regularly used toilet room, you find that the trap seal has been lost.
The LEAST common cause of this condition is
    A. evaporation of water from the trap
    B. vent blocked up
    C. high wind over roof vent
    D. self-siphonage

30. Of the following, the cleaning assignment which you would LEAST prefer to have performed during school hours is
    A. sweeping of corridors and stairs
    B. cleaning and polishing brass fixtures
    C. cleaning toilets
    D. dusting of offices, halls, and special rooms

31. BEST combustion conditions exist when the stack haze as indicated on the Ringelman chart scale is Number
    A. 1
    B. 3
    C. 5
    D. 6

32. A pop safety valve is commonly a
    A. member with a rupture section
    B. dead weight valve
    C. ball and lever valve
    D. spring-loaded valve

33. Fusible plugs used as protective devices in HRT boilers producing low pressure steam should melt at temperatures
    A. above the temperature of the steam and below the temperature of the flue gases
    B. at the same temperature as the steam
    C. above the usual temperature of both the flue gases and the steam
    D. at about the same temperature as the flue gases

34. The high low water alarm of a steam boiler is USUALLY located in the
    A. boiler
    B. gauge glass
    C. water column
    D. feedwater

35. What is an advantage of shaking grates over stationary grates?
    A. The fire can be cleaned without opening the fire door.
    B. They are warp-proof.
    C. They are usually more sturdily constructed than stationary grates.
    D. Deeper firebed can usually be maintained.

36. An ACCEPTABLE method of detecting air leaks in the setting of a boiler is
    A. placing an open flame or burning torch near the point where the leaks are suspected
    B. coating the suspected parts of the setting with heavy grease
    C. coating the suspected points of leakage with a heavy soap emulsion
    D. inspecting suspected areas of leakage with a powerful light and hand magnifier

37. In a plumbing installation, an escutcheon is a
    A. metal collar
    B. reducing tee
    C. valve
    D. single sweep

38. A leaking faucet system can be repaired by replacing the
    A. flange or the seat
    B. nipple
    C. o-ring or the packing
    D. cock

39. The abbreviation O.S. and Y, as used in plumbing, apply to a(n)
    A. hot well   B. radiator   C. injector   D. gate valve

40. Gas range piping should have a MINIMUM diameter of _____ inch.
    A. ¾   B. ½   C. ¼   D. ⅛

KEY (CORRECT ANSWERS)

1.	A	11.	C	21.	C	31.	A
2.	D	12.	D	22.	D	32.	D
3.	D	13.	B	23.	C	33.	B
4.	B	14.	C	24.	C	34.	C
5.	C	15.	B	25.	A	35.	A
6.	A	16.	C	26.	D	36.	A
7.	D	17.	A	27.	A	37.	A
8.	A	18.	A	28.	C	38.	C
9.	D	19.	A	29.	A	39.	D
10.	C	20.	B	30.	D	40.	A

EXAMINATION SECTION
TEST 1

DIRECTIONS: Each question or incomplete statement is followed by several suggested answers or completions. Select the one that BEST answers the question or completes the statement. *PRINT THE LETTER OF THE CORRECT ANSWER IN THE SPACE AT THE RIGHT.*

1. Of the following daily jobs in the schedule of a custodian, the one he should do FIRST in the morning is to

    A. hang out the flag
    B. open all doors of the school
    C. fire boilers
    D. dust principal's office

    1.____

2. When a school custodian is newly assigned to a building at the start of the school term, his FIRST step should be to

    A. examine the building to determine needed maintenance and repair
    B. meet the principal and discuss plans for operation and maintenance of the building
    C. call a meeting of the teaching and custodial staff to explain his plans for the building
    D. review the records of maintenance and operation left by the previous custodian

    2.____

3. A detergent is a material used GENERALLY for

    A. coating floors to resist water
    B. snow removal
    C. insulation of steam and hot water lines
    D. cleaning purposes

    3.____

4. A good disinfectant is one that will

    A. have a clean odor which will cover up disagreeable odors
    B. destroy germs and create more sanitary conditions
    C. dissolve encrusted dirt and other sources of disagreeable odors
    D. dissolve grease and other materials that may cause stoppages in toilet waste lines

    4.____

5. To help prevent leaks at the joints of water lines, the pipe threads are commonly covered with

    A. tar
    B. cup grease
    C. rubber cement
    D. white lead

    5.____

6. The advantage of using screws instead of nails is:

    A. They have greater holding power
    B. They are available in a greater variety than are nails
    C. A hammer is not required for joining wood members
    D. They are less expensive

    6.____

7. Of the following, the grade of steel wool that is FINEST is

    A. 00   B. 0   C. 1   D. 2

    7.____

25

8. The material used with solder to make it stick better is

   A. oakum B. lye C. oil D. flux

9. In using a floor brush in a corridor, a cleaner should be instructed to

   A. use moderately long pull strokes whenever possible
   B. make certain that there is no overlap on sweeping strokes
   C. give the brush a slight jerk after each stroke to free it of loose dirt
   D. keep the sweeping surface of the brush firmly flat on the floor to obtain maximum coverage

10. Of the following, the BEST procedure in sweeping class-room floors is:

    A. Open all windows before beginning the sweeping operation
    B. The cleaner should move forward while sweeping
    C. Alternate pull and push strokes should be used
    D. Sweep under desks on both sides of an aisle while moving down the aisle

11. PROPER care of floor brushes includes

    A. washing brushes daily after each use with warm soap solution
    B. dipping brushes in kerosene periodically to remove dirt
    C. washing with warm soap solution at least once a month
    D. avoiding contact with soap or soda solutions to prevent drying of bristles

12. An advantage of vacuum cleaning rather than sweeping a floor with a floor brush is:

    A. Stationary furniture will not be touched by the cleaning tool
    B. The problem of dust on furniture is reduced
    C. The initial cost of the apparatus is less than the cost of an equivalent number of floor brushes
    D. Daily sweeping of rooms and corridors can be eliminated

13. Sweeping compound for use on rubber tiles, asphalt tile, or sealed wood floors must NOT contain

    A. sawdust B. water C. oil soap D. floor oil

14. Of the following, the MOST desirable material to use in dusting furniture is a

    A. soft cotton cloth B. hand towel
    C. counter brush D. feather duster

15. In high dusting of walls and ceilings, the CORRECT procedure is to

    A. begin with the lower walls and proceed up to the ceiling
    B. remove pictures and window shades only if they are dusty
    C. clean the windows thoroughly before dusting any other part of the room
    D. begin with the ceiling, then dust the walls

16. When cleaning a classroom, the cleaner should

    A. dust desks before sweeping
    B. dust desks after sweeping

C. open windows wide during the desk dusting process
D. begin dusting at rows most distant from entrance door

17. Too much water on asphalt tile is objectionable MAINLY because the tile 17._____

    A. will tend to become discolored or spotted
    B. may be loosened from the floor
    C. will be softened and made uneven
    D. colors will tend to run

18. To reduce the slip hazard resulting from waxing linoleum, the MOST practical of the following methods is to 18._____

    A. apply the wax in one heavy coat
    B. apply the wax after varnishing the linoleum
    C. buff the wax surface thoroughly
    D. apply the wax in several thin coats

19. Assume that the water emulsion wax needed for routine waxing in your building is 15 gallons per month. This wax is supplied in 55-gallon drums. 19._____
    To cover your needs for a year, the MINIMUM number of drums you would have to request is

    A. two   B. three   C. four   D. six

20. In washing down the walls, the correct procedure is to start at the bottom of the wall and work to the top. 20._____
    The MOST important reason for this is:

    A. Dirt streaking will tend to be avoided or easily removed
    B. Less cleansing agent will be required
    C. Rinse water will not be required
    D. The time for cleaning the wall is less than if washing started at the top of the wall

21. In mopping a wood floor of a classroom, the cleaner should 21._____

    A. mop against the grain of the wood wherever possible
    B. mop as large an area as possible at one time
    C. wet the floor before mopping with a cleaning agent
    D. mop only aisles and clear areas and use a scrub brush under desks and chairs

22. A precaution to observe in mopping asphalt tile floors is: 22._____

    A. Keep all pails off such floors because they will leave water marks
    B. Do not wear rubber footwear while mopping these floors
    C. Use circular motion in rinsing and drying the floor to avoid streaking
    D. Never use a cleaning agent containing trisodium phosphate

23. The MOST commonly used cleansing agent for the removal of ink stains from a wood floor is 23._____

    A. kerosene   B. oxalic acid
    C. lye   D. bicarbonate of soda

24. The FIRST operation in routine cleaning of toilets and wash rooms is to

    A. wash floors
    B. clean walls
    C. clean wash basins
    D. empty waste receptacles

25. To eliminate the cause of odors in toilet rooms, the tile floor should be mopped with

    A. a mild solution of soap and trisodium phosphate in water
    B. dilute lye solution followed by a hot water rinse
    C. dilute muriatic acid dissolved in hot water
    D. carbon tetrachloride dissolved in hot water

KEY (CORRECT ANSWERS)

1. C		11. C	
2. B		12. B	
3. D		13. D	
4. B		14. A	
5. D		15. D	
6. A		16. B	
7. A		17. B	
8. D		18. D	
9. C		19. C	
10. A		20. A	

21. C
22. A
23. B
24. D
25. A

TEST 2

DIRECTIONS: Each question or incomplete statement is followed by several suggested answers or completions. Select the one that BEST answers the question or completes the statement. *PRINT THE LETTER OF THE CORRECT ANSWER IN THE SPACE AT THE RIGHT.*

1. The principal reason why soap should NOT be used in cleaning windows is: 1._____

   A. It causes loosening of the putty
   B. It may cause rotting of the wood frames
   C. A film is left on the window, requiring additional rinsing
   D. Frequent use of soap will cause the glass to become permanently clouded

2. The CHIEF value of having windows consisting of many small panes of glass is 2._____

   A. the window is much stronger
   B. accident hazards are eliminated
   C. cost of replacing broken panes is low
   D. cleaning windows consisting of small panes is easier than cleaning a window with a large undivided pane

3. Cleansing powders such as Ajax should NOT be used to clean and polish brass MAINLY because 3._____

   A. the brass turns a much darker color
   B. such cleaners have no effect on tarnish
   C. the surface of the brass may become scratched
   D. too much fine dust is raised in the polishing process

4. To remove chalk marks on sidewalks and cemented playground areas, the MOST acceptable cleaning method is: 4._____

   A. Using a brush with warm water
   B. Using a brush with warm water containing some kerosene
   C. Hosing down such areas with water
   D. Using a brush with a solution of muriatic acid in water

5. The MOST important reason for oiling wood floors is that 5._____

   A. it keeps the dust from raising during the sweeping process
   B. the need for daily sweeping of classroom floors is eliminated
   C. oiled floors present a better appearance than waxed floors
   D. the wood surface will become waterproof and stain-proof

6. After oil has been sprayed on a wood floor, the sprayer should be cleaned before storing. The usual cleaning material for this purpose is 6._____

   A. ammonia water   B. salt   C. kerosene   D. alcohol

7. The MOST desirable agent for routine cleaning of slate blackboards is 7._____

   A. warm water containing trisodium phosphate
   B. mild soap solution in warm water
   C. kerosene in warm water
   D. warm water alone

29

8. Neatsfoot oil is COMMONLY used to

   A. oil light machinery
   B. prepare sweeping compound
   C. clean metal fixtures
   D. treat covered leather chairs

Questions 9-12.

DIRECTIONS: Column I lists cleaning agents used by a custodian. Cleaning operations are given in Column II. Select the MOST common cleaning operation for the cleaning agents listed in Column I and print the letter representing your choice in the space at the right.

COLUMN I

9. Ammonia
10. Muriatic acid
11. Carbon tetrachloride
12. Trisodium phosphate

COLUMN II

A. Add water to clean marble walls
B. Remove chewing gum from wood floors
C. Wash down calcimined ceilings
D. Add to water for washing rubber tile
E. Remove stains from porcelain

13. In order to stop a faucet from dripping, the custodian would USUALLY have to replace the

   A. cap nut   B. seat   C. washer   D. spindle

14. Drinking fountains should be adjusted so that the height of the water stream is about

   A. six inches   B. three inches
   C. one inch   D. one foot

15. Before starting up the boilers each morning, the custodian or fireman should make certain

   A. all blow-off cocks and valves are open
   B. the water is at a safe level
   C. radiator and univent valves are open
   D. the main smoke damper is fully closed

16. If the radiator on a one-pipe heating system rattles or makes noise, the PROBABLE cause is

   A. steam pressure is too high
   B. steam pressure is too low
   C. steam valve is side open
   D. radiator is air bound

17. Of the following, the LARGEST size of hard coal is

   A. chestnut   B. egg   C. stove   D. pea

18. The MAIN purpose of baffle plates in a furnace is to

    A. change the direction of flow of heated gases
    B. retard the burning of gases
    C. increase combustion rate of the fuel
    D. prevent escape of flue gases through furnace openings

19. The MAIN difference between a steam header and a steam riser for a given heating system is that the

    A. riser is usually higher than the header
    B. header is larger than the riser
    C. riser is a horizontal line and the header is a vertical line
    D. header is insulated while the riser is not insulated

20. The try-cocks of steam boilers are used to

    A. act as safety valves
    B. empty the boiler of water
    C. test steam pressure in the boiler
    D. find the height of water in the boiler

21. The MOST important reason for cleaning soot from a boiler is that the

    A. soot blocks the passage of steam from the boiler
    B. soot gets into the boiler room and makes it dirty
    C. soot reduces the heating efficiency of a boiler
    D. pressure of soot is a frequent cause of the cracking of boiler tubes

22. Panic bolts are standard equipment in school buildings. Their MAIN purpose is to

    A. reduce unauthorized opening of doors and closets
    B. allow for easy opening of exit doors of the building
    C. permit rapid removal of screens from windows when a fire occurs
    D. shut storeroom doors automatically to reduce fire hazards

23. The term RPM is GENERALLY used in connection with the

    A. speed of ventilating fans
    B. water capacity of pipe
    C. heating quality of fuel
    D. electrical output of a transformer

24. A hacksaw is a light framed saw MOST commonly used to

    A. cut curved patterns in metal
    B. trim edges
    C. cut wood in confined spaces
    D. cut metal

25. A kilowatt is _____ watts.

    A. 500   B. 2,000   C. 1,500   D. 1,000

KEY (CORRECT ANSWERS)

1.	C	11.	B
2.	C	12.	D
3.	C	13.	C
4.	A	14.	B
5.	A	15.	B
6.	C	16.	D
7.	D	17.	B
8.	D	18.	A
9.	A	19.	B
10.	E	20.	D

21. C
22. B
23. A
24. D
25. D

EXAMINATION SECTION
TEST 1

DIRECTIONS: Each question or incomplete statement is followed by several suggested answers or completions. Select the one that BEST answers the question or completes the statement. *PRINT THE LETTER OF THE CORRECT ANSWER IN THE SPACE AT THE RIGHT.*

1. A boiler horse power is defined as the evaporation of _____ pounds of water per hour, from and at, 212° F.   1._____

   A. 32.0   B. 14.7   C. 34.5   D. 29.9

2. The steam drum of a water tube boiler is 16 feet long and 42" in diameter. Assuming that the normal water line is at the drum centerline, the water content of the drum under normal operating conditions is *most nearly*   2._____

   A. 700 gallons
   B. 600 gallons
   C. 400 gallons
   D. 400 cubic feet

3. In selecting a coal from its "Proximate Analysis," which of the following coals would you consider to be best suited for use in a boiler plant in a heavily populated city?   3._____

   A. 7% ash - 18% volatile matter
   B. 10% ash - 21% volatile matter
   C. 12% ash - 17% volatile matter
   D. 5% ash - 25% volatile matter

4. Which of the following types of grates should be used for ease in cleaning fires, when hand-firing large boilers with #1 buckwheat, under natural draft at heavy loads?   4._____

   A. Dumping grates
   B. Stationary grates with 3/4" air spaces
   C. Stationary grates (pin hole type)
   D. Shaking grates

5. Which of the following fuels contains the *greatest* number of heat units per pound?   5._____

   A. Hard coal
   B. No. 6 Fuel Oil
   C. Yard screenings
   D. Bituminous coal

6. In the usual water tube boiler plant using coal under natural draft, the point where the *maximum* negative draft gauge reading may be obtained is   6._____

   A. at the top of the stack
   B. at the base of the stack
   C. over the fire
   D. in the last pass

2 (#1)

7. The purpose of admitting air over the fire in a coal-fired furnace is *usually* to

   A. reduce the stack gas temperature
   B. improve the draft
   C. reduce the smoke
   D. reduce the draft

   7.____

8. With steam at a temperature of 365° F in a boiler, which of the following stack gas temperatures would you consider to be *good* usual operating practice in a plant without economizers, air preheaters and the like?

   A. 300° F   B. 500° F   C. 700° F   D. 900° F

   8.____

9. The percentage of CO_2 in the stack gases is an indication of the

   A. rate of combustion in the furnace
   B. rate at which excess air is supplied to the furnace
   C. rate of carbon monoxide production in the furnace
   D. temperature of combustion

   9.____

10. In the most usual type of large capacity oil burner using #6 oil, under "fully automatic" control, the atomization of the oil is produced MAINLY by the

    A. pressure from the pump
    B. pressure from the secondary air fan
    C. oil temperature from the heater
    D. rotation of the burner assembly by the motor

    10.____

11. Of the following, the figure which comes the *closest* to indicating the number of degree days in a normal heating season in New York City is

    A. 3000   B. 4000   C. 5000   D. 6000

    11.____

12. In which of the following steam generation methods would you expect to obtain reasonably continuous values of CO_2 *closest* to the perfect CO_2 value?

    A. Automatic stoker firing with temperature recorder
    B. Automatic stoker firing with "Hold fire timer"
    C. Automatic oil firing with "Stack switch"
    D. Automatic oil firing with "haze regulator"

    12.____

13. The loss of heat in stack gases for heavy fuel oil is HIGHEST when the

    A. CO_2 content is 12% and the stack temperature is 500°
    B. CO_2 content is 8% and the stack temperature is 600°
    C. CO_2 content is 6% and the stack temperature is 700°
    D. CO_2 content is 14% and the stack temperature is 600°

    13.____

14. A badly sooted HRT boiler under coal firing will show

    A. a higher CO_2 value than a clean boiler
    B. a lower CO_2 value than a clean boiler

    14.____

C. a higher stack temperature than a clean boiler
D. a lower draft loss than a clean boiler

15. A unit heater condensing 50 lbs. of low pressure steam per hour would be rated *most nearly* at _____ square feet E.D.R.

    A. 50   B. 100   C. 150   D. 200

16. One horsepower most nearly equals

    A. 550 ft - lbs per sec.
    B. 3300 ft - lbs per min.
    C. 55000 ft - lbs per hour
    D. 10000 ft-lbs per min.

17. An indicator card from a steam engine is MOST useful to the custodian-engineer in

    A. determining the boiler pressure
    B. determining the engine speed
    C. adjusting the valve setting
    D. computing the mechanical efficiency

18. Which one of the following statements is *most nearly* correct?

    A. A water tube boiler has the combustion gases inside the tubes
    B. A scotch marine boiler has two drums
    C. A brick set HRT boiler usually has a steel fire box
    D. The circulation in a boiler may be either gravity or forced

19. When the load on a mechanical stoker fired boiler plant furnishing steam for slide valve engine generators drops by 30%, the

    A. stoker should be shut down
    B. fan should be speeded up and the stoker slowed
    C. stoker should be speeded up and the air supply reduced
    D. stoker speed and air supply should be adjusted by reducing both

20. Which of the following statements is *most nearly* correct?

    A. All types of mechanical stokers may be used with equal efficiency under all types of boilers
    B. Most stokers are designed with a weak member
    C. The best type of stoker to use is not dependent upon the type of fuel available
    D. Advisability of installing stokers is not dependent upon the load

21. The number and size of safety valves required on a high pressure boiler is dependent upon the

    A. size of the boiler drums
    B. amount of heating surface
    C. number of pounds of fuel burned per square foot of grate per hour
    D. size of the steam main

22. In changing over a boiler from high pressure (150 lbs. per square inch) to 10 pounds per square inch, it is usually necessary to

    A. increase the size of the safety valves
    B. decrease the grate area
    C. increase the size of the feed water piping
    D. increase the size of the blow down piping

22.___

23. A boiler feed injector becomes temporarily steam bound. To correct this condition, the MOST proper action to take is to

    A. increase boiler pressure
    B. reduce suction lift
    C. wrap it with cold rags
    D. bank fire

23.___

24. If the volume of air in cubic feet per minute for combustion is represented by X, which of the following values of X would *most nearly* represent the Cfm of stack gas, under usual conditions, that an induced draft fan would have to handle?

    A. X   B. 2X   C. 3X   D. 4X

24.___

25. If the stock switch of an oil burner becomes excessively sooted, a condition *most likely* to result is

    A. continuous shutting down of the burner shortly after it starts up
    B. excessive flow of oil to the burner resulting in a smoky fire
    C. excessive fire due to failure to cut off current to the burner motor
    D. failure of the warp switch of the relay to operate

25.___

KEY (CORRECT ANSWERS)

1. C	11. C
2. B	12. D
3. A	13. C
4. A	14. C
5. B	15. D
6. B	16. A
7. C	17. C
8. B	18. D
9. B	19. D
10. D	20. B

21. B
22. A
23. C
24. B
25. A

TEST 2

DIRECTIONS: Each question or incomplete statement is followed by several suggested answers or completions. Select the one that BEST answers the question or completes the statement. *PRINT THE LETTER OF THE CORRECT ANSWER IN THE SPACE AT THE RIGHT.*

1. In high pressure electric generating plants in large buildings, heating the feed water from 70° F to 180° F with exhaust steam usually will *decrease* the fuel consumption by   1.____

   A. 5% B. 10% C. 15% D. 20%

2. The direct room radiator with a pneumatically controlled steam heating system is cold, while the adjoining rooms are heated adequately.   2.____
   Of the following, the FIRST thing you would check in the room is the

   A. steam pipe in the room before the pneumatic steam valve
   B. thermostat
   C. pneumatic steam valve
   D. thermostatic trap

3. The usual vacuum gage on a steam heating system reads in   3.____

   A. inches of vacuum
   B. feet of mercury
   C. inches of water
   D. feet of water

4. In a mechanical pressure type burner using #6 oil heated to 230°F by steam, the oil is atomized by   4.____

   A. centrifugal force
   B. steam temperature
   C. oil temperature
   D. oil pressure

5. A vaporstat with separate motor driven oil pump used on a fully automatic heavy oil burning rotary cup installation is *generally* used to   5.____

   A. keep the boiler pressure within proper limits
   B. regulate the pressure of the primary air
   C. regulate the pressure of the secondary air
   D. shut down the burner when primary air failure occurs

6. In estimating the amount of work being done by a steam driven water pump, the one of the following items which is usually the MOST important in the calculation of pump horsepower is the   6.____

   A. temperature of the water
   B. suction lift
   C. steam pressure
   D. gallons pumped

7. The term "fixture unit" *usually* refers to

   A. the number of lamp sockets in an electric lighting fixture
   B. the number of fixtures in a room or building
   C. a rate of flow
   D. amperes per second

8. When pumping water from a return tank, equipped with an automatic make up valve located below the pump, the *most probable* cause of periodic pump failures to deliver the water, would be

   A. a leak in the suction line
   B. the water was too hot
   C. there was too much water in the tank
   D. a leak in the discharge line

9. Suppose a small oil fire has broken out in the boiler room in your building. Under these circumstances, the extinguisher LEAST suitable for use is

   A. soda-acid
   B. pyrene
   C. foamite
   D. carbon dioxide

10. Of the following, a low "power factor" would MOST likely result from:

    A. Corlis valve engine operating at less than 1/2 normal rated load
    B. A large d.c. motor operating at 20% below normal speed
    C. A large induction motor operating at 60% normal rated capacity
    D. A storage battery on which the voltage has dropped to 10% below normal

11. Before putting two d.c. engine generators on the line in parallel, it is usually necessary to

    A. adjust the speeds so that both are running at exactly the same speed
    B. adjust the loads so that each machine will take its proportionate share
    C. adjust the field of the incoming unit
    D. lower the line voltage

12. Of the following, the BEST type of AC motor to use for direct connection to a timing device which must be very accurate is a

    A. synchronous motor
    B. squirrel cage motor
    C. wound rotor motor
    D. single phase capacitor motor

13. In running temporary electric wiring for a display requiring the use of 30 incandescent 50-watt lamps at the usual lighting voltage, the two main 120V loads supplying this load would carry *most nearly* _____ amps.

    A. 23.9   B. 12.5   C. 17.8   D. 9.5

14. One ton of refrigeration may be expressed MOST accurately as

    A. one ton of ice melting per hour
    B. 200 Btu per minute
    C. one horsepower-hour
    D. 970 Btu per pound

15. Which of the following statements is correct with respect to filtration plants of swimming pools:

    A. In pressure filter installations a clear well tank is always required as a reservoir of filtered water
    B. Raw water should be used to backwash filters whenever possible
    C. The rate of backwashing usually is less than the rate of filtration
    D. Alum is added to water to form a flee before the water reaches the filters

16. In the operation of a swimming pool, the statement NOT true is:

    A. All water supplied must be sterilized at the plant by chemical means
    B. The pool must be cleaned every third time that it is drained
    C. The rate of recirculation is dependent upon the size of the pool
    D. The number of persons permitted to use the pool at any one time determines the rate of recirculation

17. Of the following, the use for which central vacuum cleaning is considered LEAST effective is for

    A. cleaning walls and ceilings
    B. dusting classroom furniture
    C. cleaning boiler rooms
    D. cleaning erasers

18. An electric elevator car stalls on the ground floor of a school building. Of the following, the item you would be LEAST likely to check in your inspection is the

    A. "baby" switch
    B. floor door switch
    C. limit switch
    D. current to elevator motors

19. An examination of the water supply of the sinks of demonstration tables in science rooms reveals the use of rubber hose attachments to sink taps extending below the sink rim. Of the following, the MOST important criticism of this practice is that

    A. there is greater possibility of water waste through leakage
    B. the taps may become contaminated by contact with unclean rubber hoses
    C. a submerged inlet condition may be created resulting in back-siphonage
    D. a water hammer condition will be created by this elimination of the normal air gap

20. In an investigation of a complaint of sewer gas from a urinal in a regularly used toilet room, you find that the trap seal has been lost. The LEAST common cause of this condition is

    A. evaporation of water from the trap
    B. vents blocked up
    C. high wind over roof vent
    D. self-siphonage

21. A *check* valve in the discharge of a centrifugal pump

    A. prevents backflow to suction side
    B. keeps the pump primed at all times
    C. eliminates the need for a foot valve
    D. eliminates the need for a gate valve on the pump discharge

22. The modern multiple-circuit program instrument which automatically controls bell signals in a school *usually* includes

    A. automatic resetting of electric clocks throughout the school
    B. automatic ringing of room bells when the fire bell switch is closed
    C. prevention of manual control of schedules by eliminating manual control switches
    D. provision for automatic cutout of the schedule for any 24-hour day desired

23. Of the following, the cleaning assignment which you would LEAST prefer to have performed *during* school hours is

    A. sweeping of corridors and stairs
    B. cleaning and polishing brass fixtures
    C. cleaning toilets
    D. dusting of offices, halls and special rooms

24. A mechanical system of ventilation commonly found in schools is a unit ventilator (univent) located in each classroom. Of the following, the procedure which is NOT usually correct with respect to operation and maintenance of this unit is

    A. air pressure for operation of the unit is obtained from a central fan located in the basement
    B. when a room is to be heated in the early morning of a cold day by recirculation, the window is closed and the damper opened to the room
    C. filters coated with oil are periodically cleaned by dipping them in a solution of washing soda and hot water
    D. other radiators in the room are not normally controlled by the univent or its radiator

25. A teacher complains to you that her room is not cleaned properly each day. You have received complaints from this teacher on several occasions and have found them to be unfounded each time. The *most desirable* action to take is to FIRST

    A. tell the teacher that her room is cleaned as well as other rooms
    B. advise the teacher that she is expecting too much of the custodial staff
    C. ask the cleaner if he cleans that classroom in accordance with standard procedures
    D. visit the room to verify the complaint of the teacher

KEY (CORRECT ANSWERS)

1.	B	11.	C
2.	A	12.	A
3.	A	13.	B
4.	D	14.	B
5.	D	15.	D
6.	D	16.	B
7.	C	17.	B
8.	B	18.	C
9.	A	19.	C
10.	C	20.	A

21. A
22. A
23. D
24. A
25. D

———

EXAMINATION SECTION
TEST 1

DIRECTIONS: Each question or incomplete statement is followed by several suggested answers or completions. Select the one that BEST answers the question or completes the statement. *PRINT THE LETTER OF THE CORRECT ANSWER IN THE SPACE AT THE RIGHT.*

1. Before starting any lawn mowing, the distance between the blade and a flat surface should be measured with a ruler. This distance should be such that the cut of the grass above the ground is _____ inch(es). 1.____

   A. 1   B. 1 1/2   C. 2   D. 3

2. Strainers in a number 6 fuel oil system should be checked once a 2.____

   A. day   B. week   C. month   D. year

3. The spinning cup on a rotary cup oil burner should be cleaned once 3.____

   A. a day
   B. a week
   C. every two weeks
   D. a month

4. Terrazzo floors should be cleaned daily with a 4.____

   A. damp mop using clear water
   B. damp mop using a strong alkaline solution
   C. damp mop using a mild acid solution
   D. dust mop treated with vegetable oil

5. New installations of vinyl-asbestos floors should 5.____

   A. never be machine scrubbed
   B. be dry-buffed weekly
   C. be swept daily, using an oily compound
   D. never be swept with treated dust mops

6. Standpipe fire hose shall be inspected 6.____

   A. monthly
   B. quarterly
   C. semi-annually
   D. annually

7. All portable fire extinguishers shall be inspected once 7.____

   A. a year
   B. a month
   C. a week
   D. every 3 months

8. Soda-acid and foam-type fire extinguishers shall be discharged and recharged at least once 8.____

   A. each year
   B. every two years
   C. every six months
   D. each month

9. Elevator *safeties* under the car shall be tested once each 9.____

   A. day   B. week   C. month   D. quarter

10. Key-type fire alarms in public school buildings shall be tested

    A. daily
    B. weekly
    C. monthly
    D. quarterly

11. Combustion efficiency can be determined from an appropriate chart used in conjunction with _____ temperature and

    A. steam; steam pressure
    B. flue gas; percentage of CO_2
    C. flue gas; fuel heating value
    D. oil; steam pressure

12. In the combustion of common fuels, the major boiler heat loss is due to

    A. incomplete combustion
    B. moisture in the fuel
    C. heat radiation
    D. heat lost in the flue gases

13. The MOST important reason for blowing down a boiler water column and gauge glass is to

    A. prevent the gauge glass level from rising too high
    B. relieve stresses in the gauge glass
    C. insure a true water level reading
    D. insure a true pressure gauge reading

14. The secondary voltage of a transformer used for ignition in a fuel oil burner has a range of MOST NEARLY _____ volts to _____ volts.

    A. 120; 240
    B. 440; 660
    C. 660; 1,200
    D. 5,000; 15,000

15. Assume that during the month of April there were 3 days with an average outdoor temperature of 30° F, 7 days with 40° F, 10 days with 50° F, 3 days with 60° F, and 7 days with 65° F.
    The number of degree days for the month was

    A. 330
    B. 445
    C. 595
    D. 1,150

16. The pH of boiler feedwater is usually maintained within the range of

    A. 4 to 5
    B. 6 to 7
    C. 10 to 12
    D. 13 to 14

17. The admission of steam to the coils of a domestic hot water supply tank is regulated by a(n)

    A. pressure regulating valve
    B. immersion type temperature gauge
    C. check valve
    D. thermostatic control valve

18. The device which senses primary air failure in a rotary cup oil burner is usually called a(n)   18.____

    A. vaporstat   B. anemometer
    C. venturi   D. pressure gauge

19. The device which starts and stops the flow of oil into an automatic rotary cup oil burner is usually called a(n) _____ valve.   19.____

    A. magnetic oil   B. oil metering
    C. oil check   D. relief

20. A vacuum breaker, used on a steam heated domestic hot water tank, is usually connected to the   20.____

    A. circulating pump   B. tank wall
    C. aquastat   D. steam coil flange

21. A vacuum pump in a low pressure steam heating system which is equipped with a float switch, a vacuum switch, a magnetic starter, and a selector switch can be operated on   21.____

    A. float, vacuum, or automatic
    B. float, vacuum, or continuous
    C. vacuum, automatic, or continuous
    D. float, automatic, or continuous

22. If the temperature of the condensate returning to the vacuum pump in a low pressure steam vacuum heating system is above 180° F, the trouble may be caused by   22.____

    A. faulty radiator traps
    B. room thermostats being set too high
    C. uninsulated return lines
    D. too many radiators being shut off

23. A feedwater regulator operates to   23.____

    A. shut down the burner when the water is low
    B. maintain the water in the boiler at a predetermined level
    C. drain the water from the boiler
    D. regulate the temperature of the feedwater

24. An automatically fired steam boiler is equipped with an automatic low water cut-off. The low water cut-off is usually actuated by   24.____

    A. steam pressure   B. fuel pressure
    C. float action   D. water temperature

25. Low pressure steam or an electric heater is usually required for heating No. _____ fuel oil.   25.____

    A. 1   B. 2   C. 4   D. 6

KEY (CORRECT ANSWERS)

1. C
2. A
3. A
4. A
5. B

6. B
7. B
8. A
9. C
10. A

11. B
12. D
13. C
14. D
15. B

16. C
17. D
18. A
19. A
20. D

21. D
22. A
23. B
24. C
25. D

TEST 2

DIRECTIONS: Each question or incomplete statement is followed by several suggested answers or completions. Select the one that BEST answers the question or completes the statement. *PRINT THE LETTER OF THE CORRECT ANSWER IN THE SPACE AT THE RIGHT.*

1. A compound gauge is calibrated to read 1.____

   A. pressure only
   B. vacuum only
   C. vacuum and pressure
   D. temperature and humidity

2. In a mechanical pressure-atomizing type oil burner, the oil is atomized by using an atomizing tip and 2.____

   A. steam pressure
   B. pump pressure
   C. compressed air
   D. a spinning cup

3. A good over-the-fire draft in a natural draft furnace should be approximately _____ inches of water _____. 3.____

   A. 5.0; positive pressure
   B. 0.05; positive pressure
   C. 0.05; vacuum
   D. 5.0; vacuum

4. When it is necessary to add chemicals to a heating boiler, it should be done 4.____

   A. immediately after boiler blowdown
   B. after the boiler has been cleaned internally of sludge, scale, and other foreign matter
   C. at periods when condensate flow to the boiler is small
   D. at a time when there is a heavy flow of condensate to the boiler

5. The modutrol motor on a rotary cup oil burner burning #6 fuel oil automatically operates the primary air damper, 5.____

   A. secondary air damper, and oil metering valve
   B. secondary air damper, and magnetic oil valve
   C. oil metering valve, and magnetic oil valve
   D. and magnetic oil valve

6. The manual-reset pressuretrol is classified as a _____ Control. 6.____

   A. Safety and Operating
   B. Limit and Operating
   C. Limit and Safety
   D. Limit, Operating, and Safety

7. Sodium sulphite is added to boiler feedwater to 7.____

   A. avoid caustic embrittlement
   B. increase the pH value
   C. reduce the tendency of foaming in the steam drum
   D. remove dissolved oxygen

8. Neat cement is a mixture of cement,

   A. putty, and water
   B. and water
   C. lime and water
   D. salt, and water

9. In a concrete mix of 1:2:4, the 2 refers to the amount of

   A. sand   B. cement   C. stone   D. water

10. The word *natatorium* means MOST NEARLY a(n)

    A. auditorium
    B. playroom
    C. gymnasium
    D. indoor swimming pool

11. Plated metal surfaces which are protected by a thin coat of clear lacquer should be cleaned with a(n)

    A. abrasive compound
    B. liquid polish
    C. mild soap solution
    D. lemon oil solution

12. Wet mop filler replacements are ordered by

    A. length
    B. weight
    C. number of strands
    D. trade number

13. The BEST way to determine the value of a cleaning material is by

    A. performance testing
    B. manufacturer's literature
    C. written specifications
    D. interviews with manufacturer's salesman

14. The instructions on a container of cleaning compound states, *Mix one pound of compound in 5 gallons of water.* Using these instructions, the amount of compound which should be added to 15 quarts of water is MOST likely _____ ounces.

    A. 3   B. 8   C. 12   D. 48

15. The MOST usual cause of paint blisters is

    A. too much oil in the paint
    B. moisture under the paint coat
    C. a heavy coat of paint
    D. improper drying of the paint

16. The floor that should NOT be machined scrubbed is a(n)

    A. lobby
    B. lunchroom
    C. gymnasium
    D. auditorium aisle

17. Pick-up sweeping in a school building is the occasional removal of the more conspicuous loose dirt from corridors and lobbies.
    This type of sweeping should be done

    A. after scrubbing or waxing of floors
    B. with the aid of a sweeping compound
    C. at night after school hours
    D. during regular school hours

18. According to recommended practice, when a steam boiler is taken out of service for a long period of time, the boiler drums should FIRST be

    A. drained completely while the water is hot (above 212° F)
    B. drained completely after the water has been cooled down to 180° F
    C. filled completely without draining
    D. filled to the level of the top try cock

19. Specifications concerning window cleaners' anchors and safety belts must be in compliance with the rules and regulations outlined in the

    A. State Labor Law and Board of Standards and Appeals
    B. Building Code
    C. Fire Department Safety Manual
    D. National Protection Association

20. If it is not possible to plant new shrubs immediately upon delivery in the spring, they should be stored in a(n)

    A. sheltered outdoor area   B. unsheltered outdoor area
    C. boiler room   D. warm place indoors

21. Peat moss is generally used for its

    A. food value   B. nitrogen
    C. alkalinity   D. moisture retaining quality

22. The legal minimum age of employees engaged for cleaning windows in the state is _____ years.

    A. 16   B. 17   C. 18   D. 21

23. Pruning of street trees is the responsibility of the

    A. School Custodian Engineer
    B. Board of Education
    C. Department of Parks
    D. Borough President's Office

24. The prevention and control of vermin and rodents in a school building is PRIMARILY a matter of

    A. maintaining good housekeeping on a continuous basis
    B. periodic use of an exterminator's service
    C. calling in the exterminator when necessary
    D. cleaning the building thoroughly during school vacation

25. The MAIN classification of lumber used for construction purposes is known as _____ lumber.

    A. industrial   B. commercial
    C. finish   D. yard

KEY (CORRECT ANSWERS)

1.	C	11.	C
2.	B	12.	B
3.	C	13.	A
4.	D	14.	C
5.	A	15.	B
6.	C	16.	C
7.	D	17.	D
8.	B	18.	B
9.	A	19.	A
10.	D	20.	A

21. D
22. C
23. C
24. A
25. D

TEST 3

DIRECTIONS: Each question or incomplete statement is followed by several suggested answers or completions. Select the one that BEST answers the question or completes the statement. *PRINT THE LETTER OF THE CORRECT ANSWER IN THE SPACE AT THE RIGHT.*

1. Oil-soaked waste and rags should be

    A. deposited in a self-closing metal can
    B. piled in the open
    C. stored in the supply closet
    D. rolled up and be available for the next job

    1.____

2. Inspection for safety should be included as part of the custodian engineer's _____ inspection.

    A. daily   B. weekly   C. monthly   D. quarterly

    2.____

3. Of the following classifications, the one which pertains to fires in electrical equipment is Class

    A. A   B. B   C. C   D. D

    3.____

4. The type of portable fire extinguisher which is PARTICULARLY suited for extinguishing flammable liquid fires is the _____ type.

    A. soda-acid   B. foam
    C. pump tank   D. loaded stream

    4.____

5. Of the following liquids, the one which has the LOWEST flash point is

    A. kerosene   B. gasoline
    C. benzene   D. carbon tetrachloride

    5.____

6. When giving first aid to an injured person, which one of the following should you NOT do?

    A. Administer medication internally
    B. Send for a physician
    C. Control bleeding
    D. Treat for shock

    6.____

7. In reference to firefighting, fires are of such complexity that

    A. no plans or methods of attack can be formulated in advance
    B. the problem must be considered in advance and methods of attack formulated
    C. an appointed committee is necessary to direct fighting at the fire
    D. no planned procedures can be relied on

    7.____

8. The heat of a soldering copper should be tested

    A. with solder
    B. by holding it near kraft paper
    C. by holding it near your hand
    D. with water

    8.____

9. Safety on the job is BEST assured by

   A. keeping alert
   B. following every rule
   C. working very slowly
   D. never working alone

10. One important use of accident reports is to provide information that may be used to reduce the possibility of similar accidents.
    The MOST valuable entry on the report for this purpose is the

    A. time lost due to accident
    B. date of the occurrence
    C. injury sustained by the victim
    D. cause of the accident

11. If the directions given by your superior are NOT clear, the BEST thing for you to do is to

    A. ask to have the directions repeated and clarified
    B. proceed to do the work taking a chance on doing the right thing
    C. do nothing until some later time when you can find out exactly what is wanted
    D. ask one of the other men in your crew what he would do under the circumstances

12. Of the following procedures concerning grievances of subordinate personnel, the custodian engineer should maintain an attitude of

    A. paying little attention to little grievances
    B. being very alert to grievances and make adjustments in existing conditions to appease all personnel
    C. knowing the most frequent causes of grievances and strive to prevent them from arising
    D. maintaining rigid discipline of a nature that *smooths out* all grievances

13. Of the following, the BEST course of action to take to settle a dispute or conflict between two employees is to

    A. insist that the two employees settle the case between themselves
    B. call in each one separately and after hearing their cases presented, decide the issue
    C. bring both in for a conference at the same time and make the decision in their presence
    D. have both present their points of view and arguments in a written memoranda and on this basis make your decision

14. If, as a custodian engineer, you discover an error in your report submitted to the main office, you should

    A. do nothing, since it is possible that one error will have little effect on the total report
    B. wait until the error is discovered in the main office and then offer to work overtime to correct it
    C. go directly to the supervisor in the main office after working hours and ask him unofficially to correct the error
    D. notify the main office immediately so that the error can be corrected, if necessary

15. There are a considerable number of forms and reports to be submitted on schedule by the custodian engineer. The advisable method of accomplishing this duty is to

    A. fill out the reports at odd times during the days when you have free time
    B. schedule a definite period of the work week for completing these forms and reports
    C. assign your foreman or cleaner to handle all these forms for you and to have them available on time
    D. classify or group the forms and reports and fill out only one of each group and refer the other forms or reports to the ones completed

16. A custodian engineer can BEST evaluate the quality of work performed by custodial personnel by

    A. periodic inspection of the building's cleanliness
    B. studying the time records of personnel
    C. reviewing the building cleaning expenditures
    D. analyzing complaints of building occupants

17. Assume that you are the custodian engineer and one of your employees wants to talk with you about a grievance. Of the following actions, the LEAST desirable action for you to take is to

    A. listen sympathetically
    B. conduct the discussion openly in the presence of the workforce
    C. try to get his point of view
    D. endeavor to obtain all the facts

18. Of the following factors, the one which is LEAST important in evaluating an employee and his work is his

    A. dependability   B. quantity of work done
    C. quality of work done   D. education and training

19. Supervision of a group of people engaged in building cleaning operations should NOT include supervision of

    A. time spent in cleaning operations
    B. utilization of official rest and lunch periods
    C. cleaning methods
    D. materials used for various cleaning jobs

20. Of the following methods, the BEST one to utilize in assigning custodial personnel to clean a multi-floor school building is to

    A. allow the cleaners to pick their room or area assignments out of a hat
    B. have the supervisor make specific room or area assignments to each cleaner separately
    C. rotate room and area assignments daily according to a chart posted on the bulletin board
    D. let a different member of the group make the room or area assignments each week

21. Assume that you are the custodian engineer and that you have discovered a bottle of liquor in one of your employee's locker.
The BEST course of action to take is to

   A. fire him immediately
   B. explain to him that liquor should not be brought into a school building and that a repetition may result
   C. in disciplinary action
   D. suspend him until the end of the week and take him back only on a probational basis
   E. assemble the staff and tell them they are all equally guilty for not having reported the matter to you

22. Of the following items, the one which is the LEAST important in the preparation of a report is that the report

   A. is brief, but to the point
   B. uses the prescribed form if there is one
   C. contains extra copies
   D. is accurate

23. In order to have building employees willing to follow standardized cleaning and maintenance procedures, the supervisor must be prepared to

   A. work alongside the employees
   B. demonstrate the reasonableness of the procedures
   C. offer incentive pay for their utilization
   D. allow the employees the free use of the time saved by their adoption

24. Suppose that you are the custodian engineer and one of your employees has gross earnings of $437.10 for the week, all of which is subject to deductions at the rate of 4.8%. The amount which should be deducted from the employee's gross earnings for the week is MOST NEARLY

   A. $2.10   B. $14.70   C. $17.70   D. $20.97

25. Suppose that you are a custodian engineer and an employee works for you at the rate of $8.70 per hour with time and one-half paid for time worked after 40 hours in one week. His gross pay for working 53 hours in one week is MOST NEARLY

   A. $461.10   B. $482.10   C. $487.65   D. $517.65

KEY (CORRECT ANSWERS)

1. A
2. A
3. C
4. B
5. B

6. A
7. B
8. A
9. A
10. D

11. A
12. C
13. C
14. D
15. B

16. A
17. B
18. D
19. B
20. B

21. B
22. C
23. B
24. D
25. D

TEST 4

DIRECTIONS: Each question or incomplete statement is followed by several suggested answers or completions. Select the one that BEST answers the question or completes the statement. *PRINT THE LETTER OF THE CORRECT ANSWER IN THE SPACE AT THE RIGHT.*

1. The minimum number of gate valves usually required in a by-pass around a steam trap is 1.____

    A. 1 B. 2 C. 3 D. 4

2. A 2-inch standard steel pipe, as compared with a 2-inch extra heavy steel pipe, has the same 2.____

    A. wall thickness
    B. inside diameter
    C. outside diameter
    D. weight per linear foot

3. A short piece of pipe with a standard male pipe thread on one end and a locknut thread on the other end is usually called a 3.____

    A. close nipple
    B. tank nipple
    C. coupling
    D. union

4. Dies are used by plumbers to 4.____

    A. ream out the inside of pipes
    B. thread pipes
    C. bevel the ends of pipes
    D. make up solder joints

5. Of the following types of pipe, the one which is MOST brittle is 5.____

    A. brass
    B. copper
    C. cast iron
    D. wrought iron

6. The PRIMARY function of a trap in a drainage system is 6.____

    A. prevent gases from flowing into the building
    B. produce an efficient flushing action
    C. prevent articles accidentally dropped into the drainage system from entering the water
    D. prevent the water backing up

7. If a plumbing fixture is allowed to stand unused for a long time, its trap is opt to lose its seal by 7.____

    A. evaporation
    B. capillary action
    C. siphonage
    D. condensation

8. The pipe fitting used to connect a 1 1/4" pipe directly to a 1" pipe in a straight line is called a 8.____

    A. union B. nipple C. elbow D. reducer

9. The BEST procedure to follow when replacing a blown fuse is to

   A. immediately replace it with the same size fuse
   B. immediately replace it with a larger size fuse
   C. immediately replace it with a smaller size fuse
   D. correct the cause of the fuse failure and replace it with the correct size

10. The amperage rating of the fuse to be used in an electrical circuit is determined by the

    A. size of the connected load
    B. size of the wire in the circuit
    C. voltage of the circuit
    D. ambient temperature

11. In a 208-volt, 3-phase, 4-wire circuit, the voltage, in volts, from any line to the grounded neutral is approximately

    A. 208   B. 150   C. 120   D. zero

12. The device commonly used to change an A.C. voltage to a D.C. voltage is called a

    A. transformer   B. rectifier
    C. relay   D. capacitor or condenser

13. Where conduit enters a knock-out in an outlet box, it should be provided with a

    A. bushing on the inside and locknut on the outside
    B. locknut on the inside and bushing on the outside
    C. union on the outside and a nipple on the inside
    D. nipple on the outside and a union on the inside

14. The electric circuit to a ten kilowatt electric hot water heater which is automatically controlled by an aquastat will also require a

    A. transistor   B. choke coil
    C. magnetic contactor   D. limit switch

15. An electric power consumption meter usually indicates the power used in

    A. watts   B. volt-hours
    C. amperes   D. kilowatt-hours

16. Of the following sizes of copper wire, the one which can SAFELY carry the GREATEST amount of amperes is

    A. 14 ga. stranded   B. 12 ga. stranded
    C. 12 ga. solid   D. 10 ga. solid

17. A flexible coupling is PRIMARILY used to

    A. allow for imperfect alignment of two joining shafts
    B. allow for slight differences in shaft diameters
    C. insure perfect alignment of the joining shafts
    D. reduce fast starting of the machinery

18. The one of the following statements concerning lubricating oil which is CORRECT is: 18.____

   A. SAE 10 is heavier and more viscous than SAE 30
   B. diluting lubricating oil with gasoline increases its viscosity
   C. oil reduces friction between moving parts
   D. in hot weather, thin oil is preferable to heavy oil

19. The MAIN purpose of periodic inspections and tests made on mechanical equipment is to 19.____

   A. make the operating men familiar with the equipment
   B. keep the maintenance men busy during otherwise slack periods
   C. discover minor faults before they develop into serious breakdowns
   D. encourage the men to take better care of the equipment

20. The one of the following bearing types which is NOT classified as a roller bearing is 20.____

   A. radial   B. angular   C. thrust   D. babbit

21. In a wire rope, when a number of wires are laid left-handed into a strand and the strand laid right-handed around a hemp rope center, the wire rope is commonly known as a _____ rope. 21.____

   A. right-lay, Lang-lay
   B. left-lay, Lang-lay
   C. left-lay, regular-lay
   D. right-lay, regular-lay

22. The chemical which is NOT used for disinfecting swimming pools is 22.____

   A. ammonia
   B. calcium hypochlorite
   C. chlorine
   D. liquified chlorine

23. The one of the following V-belt sections which has the HIGHEST horsepower-per-belt rating is _____ section. 23.____

   A. A   B. B   C. C   D. D

24. An air compressor which is driven by an electric motor is usually started and stopped automatically by a(n) 24.____

   A. unloader
   B. pressure regulator valve
   C. float switch
   D. pressure switch

25. The volume, in cubic feet, of a cylindrical tank, 6 ft. in diameter x 35 ft. long is MOST NEARLY 25.____

   A. 210   B. 990   C. 1,260   D. 3,960

KEY (CORRECT ANSWERS)

1. C
2. C
3. B
4. B
5. C

6. A
7. A
8. D
9. D
10. B

11. C
12. B
13. A
14. C
15. D

16. D
17. A
18. C
19. C
20. D

21. D
22. A
23. D
24. D
25. B

EXAMINATION SECTION
TEST 1

DIRECTIONS: Each question or incomplete statement is followed by several suggested answers or completions. Select the one that BEST answers the question or completes the statement. *PRINT THE LETTER OF THE CORRECT ANSWER IN THE SPACE AT THE RIGHT.*

1. The pipe fitting that would be used to connect a 2" pipe at a 45° angle to another 2" pipe is called a(n)   1._____

    A. tee
    B. orifice flange
    C. reducer
    D. elbow

2. An instrument that measures relative humidity is called a(n)   2._____

    A. manometer
    B. interferemeter
    C. hygrometer
    D. petrometer

3. The one of the following flat drive-belts that gives the BEST service in dry places is a(n) _____ belt.   3._____

    A. rawhide
    B. oak-tanned
    C. chrome-tanned
    D. semirawhide

4. The letter representing the standard V-belt section which has the LOWEST horsepower-per-belt rating is   4._____

    A. E   B. C   C. B   D. A

5. A 6 x 19 wire rope has   5._____

    A. 6 strands
    B. 6 wires in each strand
    C. 19 strands
    D. 25 strands arranged in a 6 x 19 pattern

6. A water tank 5 feet in diameter and 30 feet high has a volume of MOST NEARLY _____ cubic feet.   6._____

    A. 150   B. 250   C. 600   D. 1200

7. The circumference of a circle with a radius of 5 inches is MOST NEARLY _____ inches.   7._____

    A. 31.3   B. 30.0   C. 20.1   D. 13.4

8. A flexible coupling should be used to connect two shafts that   8._____

    A. have centerlines at right angles to each other
    B. may be slightly out of line
    C. start and stop too fast
    D. have different speeds

9. Of the following materials used to make pipe, the one that is MOST brittle is   9._____

    A. lead   B. aluminum   C. copper   D. cast iron

10. Mechanical equipment is generally tested and inspected on regular schedules in order to

    A. avoid breakdowns
    B. train new personnel
    C. maintain inventory
    D. give employees something to do

11. The *united inches* for a pane of glass that measures 14 inches by 20 inches is

    A. 14 B. 34 C. 40 D. 54

12. The one of the following that should NOT be lubricated is a(n)

    A. spur gear train   B. motor commutator
    C. roller chain drive   D. automobile axle

13. One of the following oils that has the LOWEST viscosity is S.A.E.

    A. 70 B. 50 C. 20 D. 10W

14. A neoprene gasket would normally be used in a pipeline carrying

    A. steam   B. compressed air
    C. carbon dioxide D. light oil

15. The one of the following that would NOT be used in cleaning toilet bowls is

    A. a cleaning cloth B. oxalic acid
    C. muriatic acid   D. a detergent

16. An electric motor driven air compressor is automatically started and stopped by a

    A. thermostat   B. line air valve
    C. pressure switch D. float trap

17. The term *kilowatt hours* describes the consumption of

    A. energy   B. radiation
    C. cooling capacity D. conductance

18. AC voltage may be converted to DC voltage by means of a

    A. magnet   B. rectifier
    C. voltage regulator D. transducer

19. When replacing a blown fuse, it is BEST to

    A. install another one of slightly larger size
    B. seek the cause of the fuse failure before replacing it
    C. install another one of size smaller
    D. read the electric meters as a check on the condition of the circuit

20. A 208 volt, 3 phase, 4 wire circuit power supply has a line to grounded neutral voltage of APPROXIMATELY _____ volts.

    A. 120 B. 208 C. 220 D. 240

21. An interlock is generally installed on electronic equipment to 21._____

    A. prevent loss of power
    B. maintain VHF frequencies
    C. keep the vacuum tubes lit
    D. prevent electric shock during maintenance operations

22. A flame should not be used to inspect the electrolyte level in a lead-acid battery because 22._____
    the battery cells give off highly flammable

    A. hydrogen   B. lead oxide
    C. lithium   D. xenon

23. The purpose of the third prong in a three-prong male electric plug used in a 120 volt cir- 23._____
    cuit is to

    A. make a firm connection   B. strengthen the plug
    C. ground to prevent shock   D. act as a transducer

24. A school custodian engineer on duty is informed that an employee under his supervision 24._____
    has just been injured in the school building.
    The FIRST course of action he should take is to

    A. inform his superior
    B. aid the injured employee
    C. call a meeting of all the men
    D. order an investigation

25. In the prevention of accidental injuries, the MOST effective procedure is to 25._____

    A. install safety guards
    B. alert the workers to the hazards
    C. install lighting for easy sight
    D. eliminate the accident hazard

KEY (CORRECT ANSWERS)

1. D
2. C
3. B
4. D
5. A

6. C
7. A
8. B
9. D
10. A

11. B
12. B
13. D
14. D
15. C

16. C
17. A
18. B
19. B
20. A

21. D
22. A
23. C
24. B
25. D

TEST 2

DIRECTIONS: Each question or incomplete statement is followed by several suggested answers or completions. Select the one that BEST answers the question or completes the statement. *PRINT THE LETTER OF THE CORRECT ANSWER IN THE SPACE AT THE RIGHT.*

1. The one of the following practices that will INCREASE the possibility of school fires occurring is the

   A. using of understairs areas for storage of all kinds
   B. wiping of machinery shafts with lubricating oil
   C. ventilating of all storage spaces
   D. cleaning of lockers at frequent intervals

   1.____

2. When evaluating a building for fire hazards, the MOST important considerations are the

   A. number of stories and the height of each story
   B. location in the neighborhood and the accessibility
   C. interior lighting and the furniture
   D. number of residents and the use of the building

   2.____

3. The one of the following that is a basic safety requirement for operating a power mower is:

   A. Fill gasoline driven mower indoors
   B. Do not operate power mowers on wet grass
   C. Keep the motor running when you leave the mower unattended for only a short while
   D. Fill the tank while the engine is running

   3.____

4. You observe a red truck making a fuel delivery to your school.
   The fuel being delivered is PROBABLY

   A. gasoline   B. #2 fuel oil
   C. #4 fuel oil   D. #5 fuel oil

   4.____

5. The one of the following steps that is NOT taken when operating a carbon dioxide fire extinguisher is to

   A. carry the extinguisher to the fire and set it on the ground
   B. unhook the hose
   C. pull the pin in the valve wheel
   D. turn the valve and direct the gas to the top of the fire

   5.____

6. The BEST course of action to take to settle a job-related dispute that has arisen among two of your employees is to

   A. bring them both together, listen to their arguments, and then make a decision
   B. tell the two employees individually to settle their dispute
   C. tell both employees to submit their dispute in writing to you and then make a decision
   D. listen to the argument of each one separately and then make a decision

   6.____

7. A school custodian engineer accidentally discovers a bottle of whiskey in a staff member's desk.
   The BEST procedure for the custodian to follow is to

   A. verbally reprimand him and prefer departmental charges
   B. inform him that whiskey is not allowed in school buildings
   C. call a meeting of all the employees and tell them what you found
   D. do nothing, as you do not want to embarrass the person

8. A new employee under your supervision constantly reports late for work.
   The one of the following actions you should take FIRST is to

   A. admonish him in front of the other employees
   B. prefer charges against him
   C. transfer him to another school
   D. warn him that he must be on time

9. The one of the following procedures that is BEST to follow when it is necessary to reprimand a worker is to

   A. issue the same reprimand to all of your men
   B. avoid him so he won't feel bad
   C. speak to him privately about the matter
   D. tell him what he has done wrong immediately to teach the other employees a lesson

10. The LEAST important factor to consider when evaluating the work of an employee is

    A. his grade on his civil service test
    B. the quality of his work
    C. his resourcefulness
    D. his attendance record

11. The one of the following supervisory actions that a school custodian engineer should use LEAST often is:

    A. Make periodic reports to his superior about the work of his men
    B. Bring employees up on *charges* whenever they do anything wrong
    C. Listen to staff grievances
    D. Advise an employee concerning a personal problem

12. The MAIN supervisory responsibility of a school custodian engineer is to

    A. foster policies of the Board of Education and the parents' organizations
    B. do his job so well that the students and employees like him
    C. make assignments to his employees
    D. operate and maintain facilities in a safe and efficient manner

13. One of your employees verbally protests to you about your evaluation of his work.
    The BEST way to handle him is to

    A. advise him of your lengthy and qualified experience
    B. tell him that you do not care to talk about it
    C. explain to him how you arrived at your evaluation

D. tell him that since all of the other employees are satisfied, he should withdraw his complaint

14. A school custodian engineer will BEST keep the morales of his men high by

    A. giving praise for well-done work
    B. assigning good workers the most work
    C. personally helping each man in all the details of the man's job
    D. allowing special privileges for good work

15. In training maintenance personnel under the supervision of a school custodian engineer, the one of the following that should be given LEAST consideration by the custodian is

    A. how the training is to be given
    B. who is to be trained
    C. when the training will be given
    D. how the school principal wants them to be trained

16. The BEST attitude for a school custodian engineer to follow in his dealings with the public is to

    A. offer aid and cooperation to the public whenever possible
    B. show authority so that the public knows the limits to which they may make requests
    C. ignore the public, since the custodian has a specific job to do
    D. refer the public to a higher authority for solution of all their problems

17. The students playing in the schoolyard consistently lose rubber balls that land on the school roof. They request that you, the school custodian engineer, retrieve these balls. Of the following, the BEST procedure for you to follow is:

    A. Teach them a lesson and refuse to retrieve the balls
    B. Retrieve the balls and throw them into the incinerator
    C. One day a week retrieve the balls and return them to the students
    D. Retrieve the balls and give them to a local children's charity

18. The president of a charitable organization requests a permit to use the school building. You, the school custodian engineer, note that his same organization used the school previously and did not observe the NO SMOKING rules.
    The BEST procedure for you to follow is to

    A. deny the organization a permit since they did not obey the school regulations before
    B. issue the permit without any questions since a large group is difficult to control
    C. inform the president that if any of his members continue to disregard the no smoking rules, future permits will not be issued
    D. inform the president that if any of his members continue to disregard the no smoking rules, you will evict them from the school building

19. Due to some grievances, parents occupy your school on a weekend and refuse to leave. As the school principal is out of town and unavailable, the BEST procedure for you, the school custodian engineer on duty, is to

    A. tell your employees to vacate the school
    B. call the police department

C. cooperate with the parents on the takeover
D. lock all the people in the school

20. An organization requests a permit to use the school auditorium from the hours of 7 PM to 10 PM on a Tuesday evening. The organization also requests that its members be allowed to enter the school earlier than 7 PM and leave later than 10 PM.
The BEST procedure for you, the school custodian engineer, to follow is to

   A. inform the organization leader that the organization may only use the school from the hours of 7 PM to
   B. 10 PM
   C. issue the permit without saying anything as you want to maintain good public relations
   D. refer the matter to the school principal as you do not want to get involved
   E. ask the organization leader the reasons for the request and if the request is fair, issue the permit and let the organization do as it pleases

21. Dog owners in the neighborhood have been disregarding the *Curb Your Dog* signs and walking their dogs on your school lawn. You find that this interferes with the operation of powered lawn mowing equipment.
Your BEST procedure to follow is to

   A. put up a higher fence
   B. chase the people and dogs away
   C. tell the owners you will call the police department
   D. explain the problem to the owners and ask them to curb their dogs

22. A cleaner reports to the school custodian engineer that a particular school room is consistently messy and dirty.
The one who is equally at fault as the students for this dirty room is the

   A. students' parents
   B. regular classroom teacher
   C. student peer group
   D. cleaner for reporting the matter

23. A parent walks into a school custodian's office and starts to shout at him about a claimed injustice to her child. The PROPER procedure for the school custodian to follow is:

   A. Call the police department
   B. Summon the security guards
   C. Vacate the office
   D. Escort the parent to a guidance counselor

24. A newspaper reporter visiting a school should NORMALLY be referred to the

   A. school principal
   B. school custodian
   C. assistant superintendent of schools
   D. borough supervisor of school custodians

25. The parents of children in the neighborhood of your school complain to you that their children cannot use the school playground after school hours because the gates are closed. The BEST procedure for you to follow is to

    A. tell the parents the gates will remain closed after school hours
    B. arrange for the children to use a play street
    C. tell the parents to meet with the Board of Education on this matter
    D. try to arrange for the school gates to be open to a later hour after school hours

25.____

KEY (CORRECT ANSWERS)

1.	A	11.	B
2.	D	12.	D
3.	B	13.	C
4.	A	14.	A
5.	D	15.	D
6.	A	16.	A
7.	B	17.	C
8.	D	18.	C
9.	C	19.	B
10.	A	20.	A

21.	D
22.	B
23.	D
24.	A
25.	D

EXAMINATION SECTION
TEST 1

DIRECTIONS: Each question or incomplete statement is followed by several suggested answers or completions. Select the one that BEST answers the question or completes the statement. *PRINT THE LETTER OF THE CORRECT ANSWER IN THE SPACE AT THE RIGHT.*

1. Two cleaners swept four corridors in 24 minutes. Each corridor measured 12 feet x 176 feet.
   The space swept per man per minute was MOST NEARLY _____ square feet.

   A. 50   B. 90   C. 180   D. 350

   1._____

2. The BEST time of the day to dust classroom furniture and woodwork is

   A. in the morning before the students arrive
   B. during the morning recess
   C. during the students' lunch time
   D. immediately after the students are dismissed for the day

   2._____

3. A custodian-engineer wishes to order sponges in the most economical manner. Keeping in mind that large sponges can be cut up into many smaller sizes, the one of the following that has the LEAST cost per cubic inch of sponge is

   A. 2" x 4" x 6" sponges @ $0.24
   B. 4" x 8" x 12" sponges @ $1.44
   C. 4" x 6" x 36" sponges @ $4.80
   D. 6" x 8" x 32" sponges @ $9.60

   3._____

4. Many new products are used in new schools for floors, walls, and other surfaces. A custodian-engineer should determine the BEST procedure to be used to clean such new surfaces by

   A. referring to the Board of Education's manual of procedures
   B. obtaining information on the cleaning procedure from the manufacturer
   C. asking the advice of the mechanics who installed the new material
   D. asking the district supervisor how to clean the surfaces

   4._____

5. The one of the following chemicals that a custodian-engineer should tell a cleaner to use to remove mildew from terazzo is

   A. ammonia   B. oxalic acid
   C. sodium hypochlorite   D. sodium silicate

   5._____

6. The type of soft floor that is basically a mixture of oxidized linseed oil, resin, and ground cork pressed upon a burlap backing is known as

   A. asphalt tile   B. cork tile
   C. linoleum   D. vinyl tile

   6._____

7. The difficulty of cleaning soil from surfaces is LEAST affected by the

   A. length of time between cleanings
   B. chemical nature of the soil

   7._____

C. smoothness of the surface being cleaned
D. standard time allotted to the job

8. The one of the following cleaning agents that is generally classified as an alkaline cleaner is

   A. sodium carbonate
   B. ground silica
   C. kerosene
   D. lemon oil

9. The one of the following cleaning agents that should be used ONLY when adequate ventilation and protective measures have been taken is

   A. methylene chloride
   B. sodium chloride
   C. sodium carbonate
   D. calcium carbonate

10. Of the following, the MOST important consideration in the selection of a cleaning agent is the

    A. cost per pound or gallon
    B. amount of labor involved in its use
    C. wording of the manufacturer's warranty
    D. length of time the manufacturer has been producing cleaning agents

11. The fan motor in a central vacuum cleaner system is found to be operating at 110% of its rated capacity.
    The one of the following actions which is MOST likely to DECREASE the load on the motor is

    A. tying back several outlets in the open position on each floor
    B. moving the butterfly damper slightly toward the closed position
    C. removing ten percent of the filter bags
    D. operating the bag shaker continuously

12. The one of the following cleaning agents that should be used to remove an accumulation of grease from a concrete driveway is a(n)

    A. acid cleaner
    B. alkaline cleaner
    C. liquid soap
    D. solvent cleaner

13. The instructions for mixing a powdered cleaner in water state that you should mix three ounces of powder in a 14-quart pail three-quarters full of water.
    To obtain a mixture of EQUAL strength in a mop truck containing 28 gallons of water requires _____ ounces of powder.

    A. 6   B. 8   C. 24   D. 32

14. A resin-base floor finish USUALLY

    A. gives the highest lustre of all floor finishes
    B. should be applied in one heavy coat
    C. provides a slip-resistant surface
    D. should not be used on asphalt tile

15. The one of the following cleaning operations of soft floors that generally requires MOST   15.____
    NEARLY the SAME amount of time per 1,000 square feet as damp mopping is

    A. applying a thin coat of wax
    B. sweeping
    C. dust mopping
    D. wet mopping

16. Of the following cleaning jobs, the one that should be allowed the MOST time to com-   16.____
    plete a 1,000 square foot area is

    A. vacuuming carpets
    B. washing painted walls
    C. stripping and waxing soft floors
    D. machine-scrubbing hard floors

17. Of the following, the MOST common use of sodium silicate is to   17.____

    A. seal concrete floors   B. condition leather
    C. treat boiler water   D. neutralize acid wastes

18. Cleaners should be instructed that dust mopping is LEAST appropriate for removing light   18.____
    soil from _____ floors.

    A. terrazzo floors   B. unsealed concrete
    C. resin-finished soft   D. sealed wood

19. Of the following, the substance that should be recommended for polishing hardwood fur-   19.____
    niture is

    A. lemon oil polish   B. neat's-foot oil
    C. paste wax   D. water-emulsion wax

20. The use of concentrated acid to remove stains from ceramic tile bathroom floors USU-   20.____
    ALLY results in making the surface

    A. pitted and porous   B. clean and shiny
    C. harder and glossier   D. waterproof

21. Asphalt tile floors should be protected by coating them with   21.____

    A. hard-milled soap   B. water-emulsion wax
    C. sodium metaphosphate   D. varnish

22. Of the following, the BEST way to economize on cleaning tools and materials is to   22.____

    A. train the cleaners to use them properly
    B. order at least a three-year supply of every item in order to avoid annual price
       increases
    C. attach a price sticker to every item so that the people using them will realize their
       high cost
    D. delay ordering material for three months at the beginning of each year to be sure
       that the old material is used to the fullest extent

23. The MINIMUM amount of free chlorine that swimming pool water should contain for proper disinfection is _____ parts per million.   23._____

   A. 1.0 B. 10 C. 50 D. 500

24. The point at which swimming pool filters should be back-washed is when the difference between the inlet and outlet pressures exceeds _____ psi.   24._____

   A. 5 B. 10 C. 15 D. 20

25. An orthtolidine test is used to test a water sample to see what quantity it contains of   25._____

   A. alum B. ammonia C. chlorine D. soda ash

26. The IDEAL flue gas temperature in a rotary-cup oil-fired boiler should be equal to the steam temperature plus   26._____

   A. 50° F B. 125° F C. 275° F D. 550° F

27. The carbon dioxide reading in a boiler flue when the boiler is operating efficiently should be MOST NEARLY   27._____

   A. 0.5 inches of water
   B. 8 ounces per mol
   C. 10 psi
   D. 12 percent

28. The one of the following that PRIMARILY indicates a low water level in a steam boiler is the   28._____

   A. pressure gauge
   B. gauge glass
   C. safety valve
   D. hydrometer

29. The one of the following steps that should be taken FIRST if a safety valve on a coal-fired steam boiler pops off is to   29._____

   A. add water to the boiler
   B. reduce the draft
   C. tap the side of the safety valve with a mallet
   D. open the bottom blow-off valve

30. A device that operates to vary the resistance of an electrical circuit is USUALLY part of a _____ pressurtrol.   30._____

   A. high-limit
   B. low-limit
   C. manual-reset
   D. modulating

KEY (CORRECT ANSWERS)

1. C
2. A
3. B
4. B
5. C

6. C
7. D
8. A
9. A
10. B

11. B
12. D
13. D
14. C
15. A

16. C
17. A
18. B
19. C
20. A

21. B
22. A
23. A
24. B
25. C

26. B
27. D
28. B
29. B
30. D

———

TEST 2

DIRECTIONS: Each question or incomplete statement is followed by several suggested answers or completions. Select the one that BEST answers the question or completes the statement. *PRINT THE LETTER OF THE CORRECT ANSWER IN THE SPACE AT THE RIGHT.*

1. A solenoid valve is actuated by

    A. air pressure
    B. electric current
    C. temperature change
    D. light rays

2. A sequential draft control on a rotary-cup oil-fired boiler should operate to

    A. *open* the automatic damper at the end of the post-purge period
    B. *open* the automatic damper when the draft has increased during normal burner operation
    C. *close* the automatic damper just before the burner motor starts up
    D. *close* the automatic damper after the burner goes off and the burner cycle is completed

3. The one of the following components of flue gas that indicates, when present, that more excess air is being supplied than is being used is

    A. carbon dioxide
    B. carbon monoxide
    C. nitrogen
    D. oxygen

4. An ADVANTAGE that a float-thermostatic steam trap has over a float-type steam trap of comparable rating is that a float-thermostatic trap

    A. requires less maintenance
    B. is easier to install
    C. allows non-condensable gases to escape
    D. releases the condensate at a higher temperature

5. A pump delivers 165 pounds of water per minute against a total head of 100 feet. The water horsepower of this pump is _____ HP.

    A. 1/2 B. 2 C. 5 D. 20

6. Of the following, the BEST instrument to use to measure over-the-fire draft is the

    A. Bourdon tube gauge
    B. inclined manometer
    C. mercury manometer
    D. potentiometer

7. The temperature of the water in a steam-heated domestic hot water tank is controlled by a(n)

    A. aquastat
    B. thermostatic regulating valve
    C. vacuum breaker
    D. thermostatic trap

8. The one of the following conditions that will MOST likely cause fuel oil pressure to fluctuate is   8.____

    A. a faulty pressure gauge
    B. a clean oil-strainer
    C. cold oil in the suction line
    D. an over-tight pump drive belt

9. The cooler in a Freon 12 refrigeration system that is equipped with automatic protective devices is MOST likely to be accidentally damaged by water freeze-up when the system('s)   9.____

    A. is operating at reduced load
    B. is operating at rated load
    C. condenser water-flow is interrupted
    D. is being pumped down

10. The capacity of a water-cooled condenser is LEAST affected by the   10.____

    A. water temperature
    B. refrigerant temperature
    C. surrounding air temperature
    D. quantity of condenser water being circulated

11. Of the following chemicals used in boiler feedwater treatment, the one that should be used to retard corrosion in the boiler circuit due to dissolved oxygen is sodium   11.____

    A. aluminate   B. carbonate   C. phosphate   D. sulfite

12. The heating system in a certain school is equipped with vacuum-return condensate pumps.   12.____
    The MOST likely place for an air-vent valve to be installed in this plant is on

    A. each radiator
    B. the outlet of the domestic hot-water steam heating coil
    C. the pressure side of the vacuum pump
    D. the shell of the domestic hot water tank

13. *Priming* of a steam boiler is NOT caused by   13.____

    A. load swings
    B. uneven fire distribution
    C. too high a water level
    D. high alkalinity of the boiled water

14. A Hartford loop is used in school heating systems PRIMARILY to   14.____

    A. provide for thermal expansion of the steam distribution piping
    B. equalize the water level in two or more boilers
    C. prevent siphoning of water out of the boiler
    D. by-pass the electric fuel-oil heaters when the steam heaters are operating

15. Of the following, the MOST likely use for temperature-indicating crayons by a custodian-engineer is in   15.____

    A. checking the operation of the radiator traps
    B. replacing room thermometers that have been vandalized
    C. indicating possible sources of spontaneous combustion
    D. checking the effectiveness of an insulating panel

16. A stop-and-waste cock is GENERALLY used on   16.____

    A. refrigerant lines between the compressor and the condenser
    B. soil lines
    C. gas supply lines
    D. water lines subjected to low temperatures

17. A pressure regulating valve in a compressed air line should be PRECEDED by a(n)   17.____

    A. check valve   B. intercooler
    C. needle valve   D. water-and-oil separator

18. A house trap is a fitting placed in the house drain immediately inside the foundation wall of a building.   18.____
    The MAIN purpose of a house trap is to

    A. prevent the entrance of sewer gas into the building drainage system
    B. provide access to the drain lines in the basement for cleaning
    C. drain the basement in case of flooding
    D. maintain balanced air pressure in the fixture traps

19. The one of the following that is BEST to use to smooth a commutator is   19.____

    A. number 1/0 emery cloth   B. number 00 sandpaper
    C. number 2 steel wool   D. a safe edge file

20. The electric service that is provided to most schools in the city is nominally   20.____

    A. 208 volt-3 phase - 4 wire - 120 volts to ground
    B. 208 volt-3 phase - 3 wire - 208 volts to ground
    C. 220 volt-2 phase - 3 wire - 110 volts to ground
    D. 440 volt-3 phase - 4 wire - 240 volts to ground

21. All the fuses in an electrical panel are good but the clips on the fuse in circuit No. 1 are much hotter than the clips of the other fuses.   21.____
    Of the following, the MOST likely cause of this condition is that

    A. circuit No. 1 is greatly overloaded
    B. circuit No. 1 is carrying much less than rated load
    C. the room temperature is abnormally high
    D. the fuse in circuit No. 1 is very loose in its clips

22. Of the following, the BEST tool to use to drive a lag screw is a(n)   22.____

    A. open-end wrench   B. Stillson wrench
    C. screwdriver   D. allen wrench

23. Of the following, the one that is MOST likely to be used in landscaping work as ground cover is

    A. barberry
    B. forsythia
    C. pachysandra
    D. viburnum

24. The velocity of air in a ventilation duct is USUALLY measured with a(n)

    A. hydrometer
    B. psychrometer
    C. pyrometer
    D. pitot tube

25. The motor driving a centrifugal pump through a direct-connected flexible coupling burned out.
    When a new motor is ordered, it is IMPORTANT to specify the same NEMA frame size so that the

    A. horsepower will be the same
    B. speed will be the same
    C. conduit box will be in the same location
    D. mounting dimensions will be the same

26. A custodian-engineer should inspect the school building for safety

    A. at least once each day
    B. at least every other day
    C. at least once a week
    D. at the end of each vacation period

27. Of the following, the MOST important practice to follow in order to prevent fires in a school is to train the staff to

    A. fight fires of every kind
    B. detect and eliminate every possible fire hazard
    C. keep halls, corridors, and exits clear
    D. place flammables in fire-proof container

28. The one of the following types of portable fire extinguishers that is MOST effective in fighting an oil fire is the _____ type.

    A. soda-acid
    B. loaded-stream
    C. foam
    D. carbon dioxide

29. A custodian-engineer opens the door to the boiler room and discovers that fuel oil has leaked onto the floor and caught fire.
    Of the following, the FIRST action he should take is to

    A. notify the principal
    B. notify the Fire Department
    C. turn off the remote control switch
    D. fight the fire using a Class B extinguisher

30. The MINIMUM noise level beyond which hearing may be impaired is _____ decibels.

    A. 10
    B. 50
    C. 90
    D. 130

KEY (CORRECT ANSWERS)

1.	B	16.	D
2.	D	17.	D
3.	D	18.	A
4.	C	19.	B
5.	A	20.	A
6.	B	21.	D
7.	B	22.	A
8.	C	23.	C
9.	D	24.	D
10.	C	25.	D
11.	D	26.	A
12.	B	27.	B
13.	D	28.	C
14.	C	29.	C
15.	A	30.	C

EXAMINATION SECTION
TEST 1

DIRECTIONS: Each question or incomplete statement is followed by several suggested answers or completions. Select the one that BEST answers the question or completes the statement. *PRINT THE LETTER OF THE CORRECT ANSWER IN THE SPACE AT THE RIGHT.*

1. The combustion efficiency of a boiler can be determined with a CO_2 indicator and the   1._____

    A. under fire draft
    B. boiler room humidity
    C. flue gas temperature
    D. outside air temperature

2. A quick, practical method of determining if the cast-iron waste pipe delivered to a job has been damaged in transit is to   2._____

    A. hydraulically test it
    B. "ring" each length with a hammer
    C. drop each length to see whether it breaks
    D. visually examine the pipe for cracks

3. An electrostatic precipitator is used to   3._____

    A. filter the air supply
    B. remove sludge from the fuel oil
    C. remove particles from the fuel gas
    D. supply samples for an Orsat analysis

4. The PRIMARY cause of cracking and spalling of refractory lining in the furnace of a steam generator is *most likely* due to   4._____

    A. continuous over-firing of boiler
    B. slag accumulation on furnace walls
    C. change in fuel from solid to liquid
    D. uneven heating and cooling within the refractory brick

5. The term "effective temperature" in air conditioning means   5._____

    A. the dry bulb temperature
    B. the average of the wet and dry bulb temperatures
    C. the square root of the product of wet and dry bulb temperatures
    D. an arbitrary index combining the effects of temperature, humidity, and movement

6. The piping in all buildings having dual water distribution systems should be identified by a color coding of _____ for potable water lines and _____ for non-potable water lines.   6._____

    A. green; red
    B. green; yellow
    C. yellow; green
    D. yellow; red

7. The breaking of a component of a machine subjected to excessive vibration is called   7._____

    A. tensile failure
    B. fatigue failure
    C. caustic embrittlement
    D. amplitude failure

8. The TWO MOST important factors to be considered in selecting fans for ventilating systems are

   A. noise and efficiency
   B. space available and weight
   C. first cost and dimensional bulk
   D. construction and arrangement of drive

   8.____

9. In the modern power plant deaerator, air is removed from water to

   A. reduce heat losses in the heaters
   B. reduce corrosion of boiler steel due to the air
   C. reduce the load of the main condenser air pumps
   D. prevent pumps from becoming vapor bound

   9.____

10. The abbreviations BOD, COD, and DO are associated with

    A. flue gas analysis
    B. air pollution control
    C. boiler water treatment
    D. water pollution control

    10.____

11. The piping of a newly installed drainage system should be tested upon completion of the rough plumbing with a head of water of NOT LESS THAN _____ feet.

    A. 10   B. 15   C. 20   D. 25

    11.____

12. Of the following statements concerning aquastats, the one which is CORRECT is:

    A. Aquastats may be obtained with either a narrow or wide range of settings
    B. Aquastats have a mercury tube switch which is controlled by the stack switch
    C. An aquastat is a device used to shut down the burner in the event of low water in the boiler
    D. An aquastat should be located about 4 inches above the normal water line of the boiler

    12.____

13. The SAFEST way to protect the domestic water supply from contamination by sewage or non-potable water is to insert

    A. air gaps
    B. swing connections
    C. double check valves
    D. tanks with overhead discharge

    13.____

14. The MAIN function of a back-pressure valve which is sometimes found in the connection between a water drain pipe and the sewer system is to

    A. equalize the pressure between the drain pipe and the sewer
    B. prevent sewer water from flowing into the drain pipe
    C. provide pressure to enable waste to reach the sewer
    D. make sure that there is not too much water pressure in the sewer line

    14.____

15. Boiler water is neutral if its pH value is

    A. 0   B. 1   C. 7   D. 14

    15.____

16. A domestic hot water mixing or tempering valve should be preceded in the hot water line by a

    A. strainer
    B. foot valve
    C. check valve
    D. steam trap

17. Between a steam boiler and its safety valve there should be

    A. no valve of any type
    B. a gate valve of the same size as the safety valve
    C. a swing check valve of at least the same size as the safety valve
    D. a cock having a clear opening equal in area to the pipe connecting the boiler and safety valve

18. A diagram of horizontal plumbing drainage lines should have cleanouts shown

    A. at least every 25 feet
    B. at least every 100 feet
    C. wherever a basin is located
    D. wherever a change in direction occurs

19. When a Bourdon gauge is used to measure steam pressures, some form of siphon or water seal must be maintained.
    The reason for this is to

    A. obtain "absolute" pressure readings
    B. prevent steam from entering the gage
    C. prevent condensate from entering the gage
    D. obtain readings below atmospheric pressure

20. In a closed heat exchanger, oil is cooled by condensate which is to be returned to a boiler. In order to avoid the possibility of contaminating the condensate with oil should a tube fail in the oil cooler, it would be good practice to

    A. cool the oil by air instead of water
    B. treat the condensate with an oil solvent
    C. keep the oil pressure in the exchanger higher than the water pressure
    D. keep the water pressure in the exchanger higher than the oil pressure

21. A radiator thermostatic trap is used on a vacuum return type of heating system to

    A. release the pocketed air only
    B. reduce the amount of condensate
    C. maintain a predetermined radiator water level
    D. prevent the return of live steam to the return line

22. According to the color coding of piping, fire protection piping should be painted

    A. green   B. yellow   C. purple   D. red

23. The MAIN purpose of a standpipe system is to

    A. supply the roof water tank
    B. provide water for firefighting

4 (#1)

    C. circulate water for the heating system
    D. provide adequate pressure for the water supply

24. The name "Saybolt" is associated with the measurement of

    A. viscosity   B. Btu content
    C. octane rating   D. temperature

25. Recirculation of conditioned air in an air-conditioned building is done MAINLY to

    A. reduce refrigeration tonnage required
    B. increase room entrophy
    C. increase air specific humidity
    D. reduce room temperature below the dewpoint

26. In a plumbing installation, vent pipes are GENERALLY used to

    A. prevent the loss of water seal from traps by evaporation
    B. prevent the loss of water seal due to several causes other than evaporation
    C. act as an additional path for liquids to flow through during normal use of a plumbing fixture
    D. prevent the backflow of water in a cross-connection between a drinking water line and a sewage line

27. The designation "150 W" cast on the bonnet of a gate valve is an indication of the

    A. water working temperature
    B. water working pressure
    C. area of the opening in square inches
    D. weight of the valve in pounds

28. In the city, the size soil pipe necessary in a sewage drainage system is determined by the

    A. legal occupancy of the building
    B. vertical height of the soil line
    C. number of restrooms connected to the soil line
    D. number of "fixture units" connected to the soil line

29. Fins or other extended surfaces are used on heat exchanger tubes when

    A. the exchanger is a water-to-water exchanger
    B. water is on one side of the tube and condensing steam on the other side
    C. the surface coefficient of heat transfer on both sides of the tube is high
    D. the surface coefficient of heat transfer on one side of the tube is low compared to the coefficient on the other side of the tube

30. A fusible plug may be put in a fire tube boiler as an emergency device to indicate low water level. The fusible plug is installed so that under normal operating conditions,

    A. both sides are exposed to steam
    B. one side is exposed to water and the other side to steam
    C. one side is exposed to steam and the other side to hot gases
    D. one side is exposed to the water and the other side to hot gases

31. Extra strong wrought-iron pipe, as compared to standard wrought-iron pipe of the same nominal size, has

    A. the same outside diameter but a smaller inside diameter
    B. the same inside diameter but a larger outside diameter
    C. a larger outside diameter and a smaller inside diameter
    D. larger inside and outside diameters

32. Fans may be rated on a dynamic or a static efficiency basis. The dynamic efficiency would *probably* be

    A. lower in value because of the energy absorbed by the air velocity
    B. the same as the static in the case of centrifugal blowers running at various speeds
    C. the same as the static in the case of axial flow blowers running at various speeds
    D. higher in value than the static

33. The function of the stack relay in an oil burner installation is to

    A. regulate the draft over the fire
    B. regulate the flow of fuel oil to the burner
    C. stop the motor if the oil has not ignited
    D. stop the motor if the water or steam pressure is too high

34. The type of centrifugal pump which is inherently balanced for hydraulic thrust is the

    A. double suction impeller type
    B. single suction impeller type
    C. single stage type
    D. multistage type

35. The specifications for a job using sheet lead calls for "4-lb. sheet lead." This means that each sheet should weigh

    A. 4 lbs.   B. 4 lbs. per square
    C. 4 lbs. per square foot   D. 4 lbs. per cubic inch

36. The total cooling load design conditions for a building are divided for convenience into two components.
    These are:

    A. infiltration and radiation
    B. sensible heat and latent heat
    C. wet and dry bulb temperatures
    D. solar heat gain and moisture transfer

37. The function of a Hartford loop used on some steam boilers is to

    A. limit boiler steam pressure
    B. limit temperature of the steam
    C. prevent high water levels in the boiler
    D. prevent back flow of water from the boiler into the return main

38. Vibration from a ventilating blower can be prevented from being transmitted to the duct work by

   A. installing straighteners in the duct
   B. throttling the air supply to the blower
   C. bolting the blower tightly to the duct
   D. installing a canvas sleeve at the blower outlet

39. A specification states that access panels to suspended ceiling will be of metal. The MAIN reason for providing access panels is to

   A. improve the insulation of the ceiling
   B. improve the appearance of the ceiling
   C. make it easier to construct the building
   D. make it easier to maintain the building

40. A plumber on a job reports that the steamfitter has installed a 3" steam line in a location at which the plans show the house trap. On inspecting the job, you should

   A. tell the steamfitter to remove the steam line
   B. study the condition to see if the house trap can be relocated
   C. tell the plumber and steamfitter to work it out between themselves and then report to you
   D. tell the plumber to find another location for the trap because the steamfitter has already completed his work

41. In the installation of any heating system, the MOST important consideration is that

   A. all elements be made of a good grade of cast iron
   B. all radiators and connectors be mounted horizontally
   C. the smallest velocity of flow of heating medium be used
   D. there be proper clearance between hot surfaces and surrounding combustible material

42. Which one of the following is the PRIMARY object in drawing up a set of specifications for materials to be purchased?

   A. Control of quality
   B. Outline of intended use
   C. Establishment of standard sizes
   D. Location and method of inspection.

43. The drawing which should be used as a LEGAL reference when checking completed construction work is the _____ drawing.

   A. contract
   B. assembly
   C. working or shop
   D. preliminary

Questions 44-50.

DIRECTIONS: Questions 44 through 50 refer to the plumbing drawing shown below.

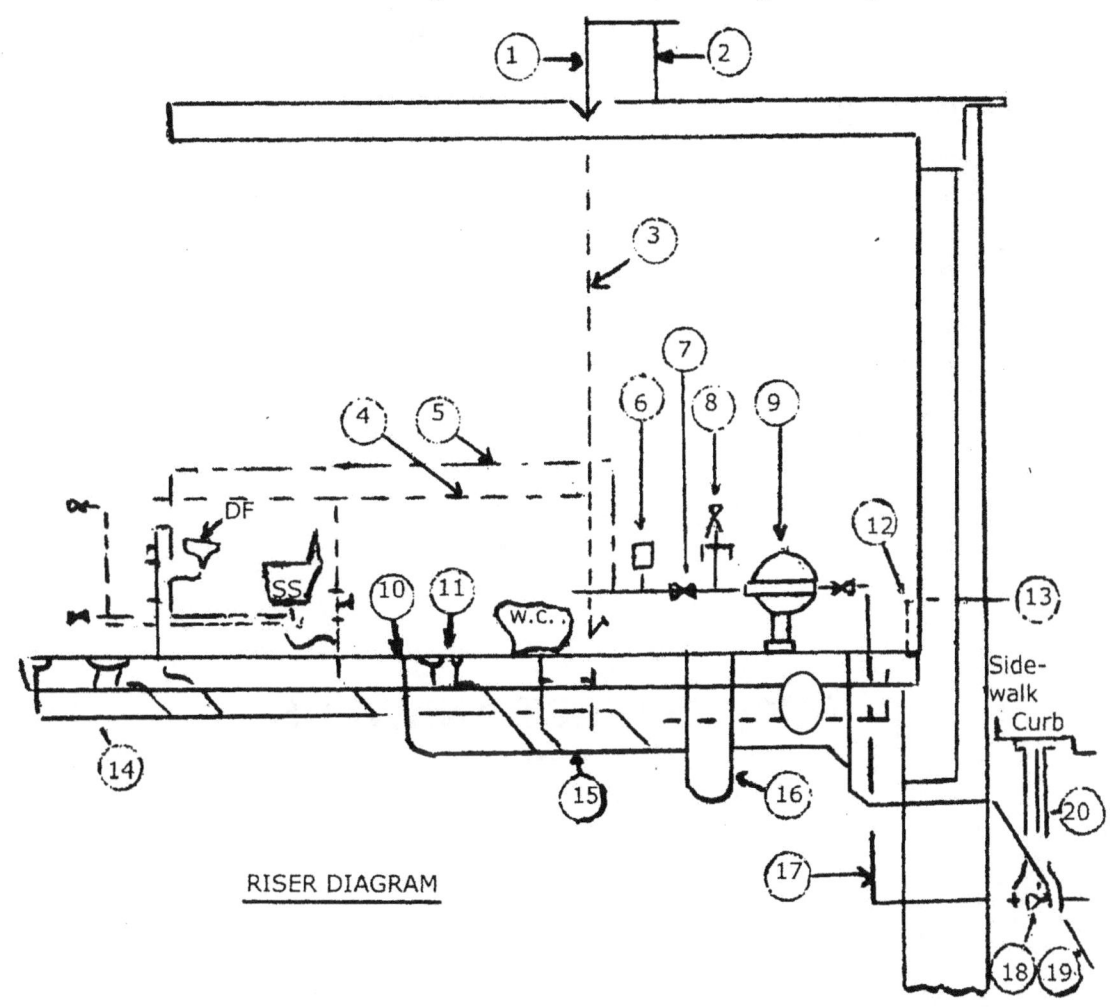

RISER DIAGRAM

44. According to the building code, the MINIMUM diameter of No. 1 and its minimum height, No. 2 respectively, are

    A. 2" and 12"   B. 3" and 18"
    C. 4" and 24"   D. 6" and 36"

44.____

45. No. 6 is a

    A. relief valve   B. shock absorber
    C. testing connection   D. drain

45.____

46. No. 9 is a

    A. strainer   B. float valve
    C. meter   D. pedestal

46.____

47. No. 11 is a

    A. floor drain   B. cleanout
    C. trap   D. vent connection

47.____

48. No. ⓭ is a

   A. standpipe
   C. sprinkler head
   B. air inlet
   D. cleanout

49. The size of No. ⓰ is

   A. 2" x 2"
   C. 3" x 3"
   B. 2" x 3"
   D. 4" x 4"

50. No. ⓲ is a

   A. pressure reducing valve
   B. butterfly valve
   C. curb cock
   D. sprinkler head

KEY (CORRECT ANSWERS)

1. C	11. A	21. D	31. A	41. D
2. B	12. C	22. D	32. D	42. A
3. C	13. A	23. B	33. C	43. A
4. D	14. B	24. A	34. A	44. C
5. D	15. C	25. A	35. C	45. B
6. B	16. A	26. B	36. B	46. C
7. B	17. A	27. B	37. D	47. A
8. A	18. D	28. D	38. D	48. B
9. B	19. B	29. D	39. D	49. D
10. D	20. D	30. D	40. B	50. C

EXAMINATION SECTION
TEST 1

DIRECTIONS: Each question or incomplete statement is followed by several suggested answers or completions. Select the one that BEST answers the question or completes the statement. *PRINT THE LETTER OF THE CORRECT ANSWER IN THE SPACE AT THE RIGHT.*

Questions 1-3.

DIRECTIONS: Questions 1 through 3, inclusive, are to be answered in accordance with the American Standard Graphical Symbols for Pipe Fittings, Valves, and Piping and American Standard Graphical Symbols for Heating, Ventilating and Air Conditioning.

1. The symbol ⊙― shown on a piping drawing represents a _____ elbow.

   A. turned down
   B. reducing
   C. long radius
   D. turned up

2. The symbol ―▭― shown on a heating drawing represents a(n)

   A. expansion joint
   B. hanger or support
   C. heat exchanger
   D. air eliminator

3. The symbol ―⋈― shown on a piping drawing represents a _____ gate valve.

   A. welded
   B. flanged
   C. screwed
   D. bell and spigot

4. The MAIN purpose for the inspection of plant equipment, buildings, and facilities is to

   A. determine the quality of maintenance work of all the trades
   B. prevent the overstocking of equipment and materials used in maintenance work
   C. forecast normal maintenance jobs for existing equipment, buildings, and facilities
   D. prevent unscheduled interruptions of operating equipment and excessive deterioration of buildings and facilities

5. Of the following devices, the one that is used to determine the rating, in cubic feet per minute, of a unit ventilator is a(n)

   A. psychrometer
   B. pyrometer
   C. anemometer
   D. manometer

6. A number of 4' x 6' skids loaded with material are to be stored. Assume that the total weight of each loaded skid is 1200 pounds and that the maximum allowable floor load is 280 lbs. per sq. ft.
   The MAXIMUM number of skids that can be stacked vertically without exceeding the MAXIMUM allowable floor load is

   A. 4
   B. 5
   C. 6
   D. 7

7. Specifications which contain the term *slump test* would MOST likely refer to

   A. lumber B. paint C. concrete D. water

8. Of the following sizes of copper conductors, the one which has the LEAST current-carrying capacity is _____ AWG.

   A. 000 B. 0 C. 8 D. 12

9. The size of a steel beam is shown on a steel drawing as W 8 x 15.
   In accordance with the latest edition of the Steel Construction Manual of the American Institute of Steel Construction, the number 8 in W 8 x 15 represents the beam's *approximate*

   A. depth
   C. width
   B. flange thickness
   D. web thickness

10. For expediting control functions such as work methods, planning, scheduling, and work measurement, EQUIPMENT RECORDS must contain specific data.
    Of the following, the data which is NOT usually indicated on an EQUIPMENT RECORD card is

    A. machinery and parts specifications numbers
    B. a breakdown history
    C. a preventive maintenance history
    D. salvage value on the open market

11. Refrigeration piping, valves, fittings, and related parts used in the construction and installation of refrigeration systems shall conform to the

    A. American Society of Mechanical Engineers Boiler and Pressure Vessel Code
    B. American Standards Association Code for Pressure Piping
    C. Pipe Fabrication Institute Standards
    D. Underwriters Laboratory Standards

12. The maintenance term *downtime* means MOST NEARLY the

    A. period of time in which a machine is out of service
    B. routine replacement of parts or materials to a piece of equipment
    C. labor required for clean-up of equipment to insure its proper operation
    D. maintenance work which is confined to checking, adjusting, and lubrication of equipment

13. A supplier quotes a list price of $172.00 less 15 and 10 percent for twelve tools.
    The ACTUAL cost for these twelve tools is MOST NEARLY

    A. $146 B. $132 C. $129 D. $112

14. Of the following colors of electrical conductor coverings, the one which indicates a conductor used SOLELY for grounding portable or fixed electrical equipment is

    A. blue B. green C. red D. black

15. A *medium duty* type of scaffold is one on which the working load on the platform surface must NOT exceed _____ pounds per square foot.

    A. 50 B. 70 C. 90 D. 110

3 (#1)

16. Assume that a mechanic is using a powder-actuated tool and the cartridge misfires. According to recommended safe practices regarding a misfired cartridge, the FIRST course of action the mechanic should take is to

    A. place the misfired cartridge carefully into a metal container filled with water
    B. carefully reload the tool with the misfired cartridge and try it again
    C. immediately bury the misfired cartridge at least two feet in the ground
    D. remove the wadding from the misfired cartridge and empty the powder into a pail of sand

17. The ratings used in classifying fire resistant building construction materials are MOST frequently expressed in

    A. Btu's   B. hours   C. temperatures   D. pounds

18. The only legible portion of the nameplate on a piece of equipment reads: *208 volts, 3 phase, 10 H.P.*
    This data would MOST NEARLY indicate that the piece of equipment is a(n)

    A. amplifier   B. fixture ballast
    C. motor   D. rectifier

19. Of the following items relating to the maintenance of roofs, the one which is of the LEAST value in a preventive maintenance program for roofs is knowledge of the

    A. roofing specifications   B. application procedures
    C. process of deterioration   D. frequency of rainstorms

20. In an oxyacetylene cutting outfit, the color of the hose that is connected to the oxygen cylinder is USUALLY

    A. white   B. yellow   C. red   D. green

21. Assume that a welding generator is to be used to weld partitions made of 18 gauge steel. Of the following settings, the BEST one to use would be a _____ setting of voltage and a _____ setting of amperage.

    A. high; high   B. high; low   C. low; high   D. low; low

22. According to the administrative code, when color marking is used, potable water lines shall be painted

    A. yellow   B. blue   C. red   D. green

23. A set of mechanical plan drawings is drawn to a scale of 1/8" = 1 foot.
    If a length of pipe measures 15 7/16" on the drawing, the ACTUAL length of the pipe is _____ feet.

    A. 121.5   B. 122.5   C. 123.5   D. 124.5

24. A portion of a specification states: *Concrete, other than that placed under water, should be compacted and worked into place by spading or puddling.*
    The MAIN reason why *spading and puddling* is required is to

    A. insure that all water in the concrete mix is brought to the surface
    B. eliminate stone pockets and large bubbles of air

C. provide a means to obtain a spade full of concrete for test purposes
D. make allowances for *bleeding and segregation* of the concrete

25. Assume that the following statement appears in a construction contract: *Payment will be made for the number of pounds of bar reinforcement incorporated in the work as shown on the plans.*
This type of contract is MOST likely

    A. cost plus   B. lump sum   C. subcontract   D. unit price

26. Partial payments to outside contractors are USUALLY based on the

    A. breakdown estimate submitted after the contract was signed
    B. actual cost of labor and material plus overhead and profit
    C. estimate of work completed which is generally submitted periodically
    D. estimate of material delivered to the job

27. Building contracts usually require that estimates for changes made in the field be submitted for approval before the work can start.
The MAIN reason for this requirement is to

    A. make sure that the contractor understands the change
    B. discourage such changes
    C. keep the contractor honest
    D. enable the department to control its expenses

28. An *addendum* to contract specifications means MOST NEARLY

    A. a substantial completion payment to the contractor for work almost completed
    B. final acceptance of the work by authorities of all contract work still to be done
    C. additional contract provisions issued in writing by authorities prior to receipt of bids
    D. work other than that required by the contract at the time of its execution

29. Of the following terms, the one which is usually NOT used to describe the types of payments to outside contractors for work done is the _____ payment.

    A. partial payment   B. substantial completion
    C. final   D. surety

30. Of the following metals, the one which is a ferrous metal is

    A. cast iron   B. brass   C. bronze   D. babbit

31. Assume that you have assigned six mechanics to do a job that must be finished in four days. At the end of three days, your men have completed only two-thirds of the job. In order to complete the job on time and because the job is such that it cannot be speeded up, you should assign a MINIMUM of _____ extra men.

    A. 3   B. 4   C. 5   D. 6

32. Of the following traps, the one which is NORMALLY used to retain steam in a heating unit or piping is the _____ trap.

    A. P   B. running   C. float   D. bell

33. Of the following materials, the one which is a convenient and powerful adhesive for cementing tears in canvas jackets that are wrapped around warm pipe insulation is   33._____

    A. cylinder oil
    B. wheat paste
    C. water glass
    D. latex paint

34. Pipe chases should be provided with an access door PRIMARILY to provide means to   34._____

    A. replace piping lines
    B. either inspect or manipulate valves
    C. prevent condensate from forming on the pipes
    D. check the chase for possible structural defects

35. Electric power is measured in   35._____

    A. volts   B. amperes   C. watts   D. ohms

KEY (CORRECT ANSWERS)

1.	D	16.	A
2.	A	17.	B
3.	B	18.	C
4.	D	19.	D
5.	C	20.	D
6.	B	21.	B
7.	C	22.	D
8.	D	23.	C
9.	A	24.	B
10.	D	25.	D
11.	B	26.	C
12.	A	27.	D
13.	B	28.	C
14.	B	29.	D
15.	A	30.	A

31. A
32. C
33. C
34. B
35. C

TEST 2

DIRECTIONS: Each question or incomplete statement is followed by several suggested answers or completions. Select the one that BEST answers the question or completes the statement. *PRINT THE LETTER OF THE CORRECT ANSWER IN THE SPACE AT THE RIGHT.*

1. The HIGHEST quality tools should

    A. always be bought
    B. never be bought
    C. be bought when they offer an overall advantage
    D. be bought only for foreman

2. Master keys should have no markings that will identify them as such.
   This statement is

    A. *false;* it would be impossible to keep records about them without such markings
    B. *true;* markings are subject to alteration and vandalization
    C. *false;* without such markings, they would be too lightly regarded by those to whom issued
    D. *true;* markings would only highlight their value to a potential wrongdoer

3. For a foreman to usually delay for a few weeks handling grievances his men make is a

    A. *poor* practice; it can affect the morale of the men
    B. *good* practice; it will discourage grievances
    C. *poor* practice; the causes of grievances usually disappear if action is delayed
    D. *good* practice; most employee grievances are not justified

4. Whenever an important change in procedure is contemplated, some foremen make a point of discussing the matter with their subordinates in order to get their viewpoint on the proposed change.
   In general, this practice is advisable MAINLY for the reason that

    A. subordinates can often see the effects of procedural changes more clearly than foremen
    B. the foreman has an opportunity to explain the advantages of the new procedure
    C. future changes will be welcomed if subordinates are kept informed
    D. participation in work planning helps to build a spirit of cooperation among employees

5. An estimate of employee morale could LEAST effectively be appraised by

    A. checking accident and absenteeism records
    B. determining the attitudes of employees toward their job
    C. examining the number of requests for emergency leaves of absence
    D. reviewing the number and nature of employee suggestions

6. Assume that you are a foreman and that a visitor at the job site asks you what your crew is doing.
   You should

A. respectfully decline to answer since all questions must be answered by the proper authority
B. answer as concisely as possible but discourage undue conversation
C. refer the man to your superiors
D. give the person complete details of the job

7. Cooperation can BEST be obtained from the general public by

    A. siding with them whenever they have a complaint
    B. sticking carefully to your work and ignoring everything else
    C. explaining the department's objectives and why the public must occasionally be temporarily inconvenienced
    D. listening politely to their complaints and telling them that the complaints will be forwarded to the main office

8. While you are working for the city, a man says to you that one of the rules of your job doesn't make sense and he gets mad.
You should say to him

    A. Leave me alone so I can get my work done
    B. Everyone must follow the rules
    C. Let me tell you the reason for the rule
    D. I'm only doing my job so don't get mad at me

9. One approach to preparing written reports to superiors is to present first the conclusions and recommendations and then the data on which the conclusions and recommendations are based.
The use of this approach is BEST justified when the

    A. data completely support the conclusions and recommendations
    B. superiors lack the specific training and experience required to understand and interpret the data
    C. data contain more information than is required for making the conclusions and recommendations
    D. superiors are more interested in the conclusions and recommendations than in the data

10. The MOST important reason why separate paragraphs might be used in writing a report is that this

    A. makes it easier to understand the report
    B. permits the report to be condensed
    C. gives a better appearance to the report
    D. prevents accidental elimination of important facts

11. On a drawing, the following standard cross-section represents MOST NEARLY

    A. sand   B. concrete   C. earth   D. rock

12. On a drawing, the following standard cross-section represents MOST NEARLY

    A. malleable iron B. steel
    C. bronze D. lead

13. On a piping plan drawing, the symbol represents a 90° _____ elbow.

    A. flanged B. screwed
    C. bell and spigot D. welded

14. On a drawing, the symbol ⋘⋘ represents

    A. stone B. steel C. glass D. wood

15. On a heating piping drawing, the symbol ─/─/─/─ represents piping.

    A. high-pressure steam B. medium-pressure steam
    C. low-pressure D. hot water supply

16. Of the following devices, the one that is LEAST frequently used to attach a piece of equipment to concrete or masonry walls is a(n)

    A. carriage bolt B. through bolt
    C. lag screw D. expansion bolt

17. A vapor barrier is usually installed in conjunction with

    A. drainage piping B. roof flashing
    C. building insulation D. wood sheathing

Questions 18-20.

DIRECTIONS: Questions 18 through 20 are to be answered in accordance with the following table

	Man Days Borough 1 Oct. Nov.	Man Days Borough 2 Oct. Nov.	Man Days Borough 3 Oct. Nov.	Man Days Borough 4 Oct. Nov.
Carpenter	70 100	35 180	145 205	120 85
Plumber	95 135	195 100	70 130	135 80
House Painter	90 90	120 80	85 85	95 195
Electrician	120 110	135 155	120 95	70 205
Blacksmith	125 145	60 180	205 145	80 125

18. In accordance with the above table, if the average daily pay of the five trades listed above is $47.50, the approximate labor cost of work done by the five trades during the month of October for Borough 1 is MOST NEARLY

    A. $22,800 B. $23,450 C. $23,750 D. $26,125

19. In accordance with the above table, the Borough which MOST NEARLY made up 22.4% of the total plumbing work force for the month of November is Borough

    A. 1 B. 2 C. 3 D. 4

20. In accordance with the above table, the average man days per month per Borough spent on electrical work for all Boroughs combined is MOST NEARLY

    A. 120 B. 126 C. 130 D. 136

21. Of the following percentages of carbon, the one that would indicate a medium carbon steel is

    A. 0.2% B. 0.4% C. 0.8% D. 1.2%

22. A *screw pitch gage* measures only the

    A. looseness of threads
    B. tightness of threads
    C. number of threads per inch
    D. gage number

23. Assume that you are to make an inspection of a building to determine the need for painting.
    Of the following tools, the one which is LEAST needed to aid you in your inspection is a

    A. sharp penknife   B. putty knife
    C. lightweight tack hammer   D. six-foot rule

24. A *slump test* for concrete is used MAINLY to measure the concrete's

    A. strength B. consistency C. flexibility D. porosity

25. Specifications which contain the term *kiln dried* would MOST likely refer to

    A. asphalt shingles   B. brick veneer
    C. paint lacquer   D. lumber

26. In accordance with established jurisdictional work procedures among the trades, the person you would assign to replace a malfunctioning fire sprinkler head would be a

    A. plumber B. laborer C. housesmith D. steamfitter

27. Of the following types of union shops, the one which is illegal under the Taft-Hartley Law is the _____ shop.

    A. closed   B. open
    C. union   D. union representative

28. Of the following types of contracts, the one that in city work would MOST likely be limited to emergency work *only* is

    A. lump-sum
    B. unit-price
    C. cost-plus
    D. partial cost-plus and lump-sum

29. Of the following qualifications of outside work contractors, the one which is the LEAST important requirement for determining eligible contractors is

    A. availability
    B. size of work force
    C. experience
    D. location of business

30. Of the following piping materials, the one that combines the physical strength of mild steel with the corrosion resistance of gray iron is

    A. grade A steel
    B. grey cast iron
    C. welded wrought iron
    D. ductile iron

31. Assume that a can of red lead paint needs to be thinned slightly. Of the following, the one that should be used is

    A. turpentine
    B. lacquer thinner
    C. water
    D. alcohol

32. Assume that a trench is 42" wide, 5' deep, and 100' long. If the unit price of excavating the trench is $35 per cubic yard, the cost of excavating the trench is MOST NEARLY

    A. $2,275   B. $5,110   C. $7,000   D. $21,000

33. Of the following uses, the one for which a bituminous compound would usually be used is to

    A. prevent corrosion of buried steel tanks
    B. increase the strength of concrete
    C. caulk water pipes
    D. paint inside wood columns

34. An electrical drawing is drawn to a scale of 1/4" = 1'.
    If a length of conduit on the drawing measures 7 3/8", the actual length of the conduit, in feet, is MOST NEARLY

    A. 7.5'   B. 15.5'   C. 22.5'   D. 29.5'

35. Of the following steam heating systems, the one that operates under both vacuum and low pressure conditions, without using a vacuum pump, is generally known as a _____ system.

    A. one pipe low pressure
    B. vacuum
    C. vapor
    D. high pressure

36. Of the following valve trim symbols, the one which designates a valve trim made of monel material is

    A. 8-18   B. NI-CU   C. SM   D. MI

37. A replacement part for a piece of equipment is to be made of S.A.E. 4047 steel. This material is MOST likely a _____ steel.

    A. wrought
    B. nickel
    C. chrome-vanadium
    D. molybdenum

38. A metallic underground water piping system is to be used as a means of grounding. Of the following statements concerning use of this system, the one that is MOST NEARLY CORRECT is that this use is

   A. not permitted
   B. permitted where available
   C. absolutely required
   D. permitted only in certain cases

38.____

39. For pipe sizes up to 8", schedule 40 pipe is identical to _____ pipe.

   A. standard
   B. extra strong
   C. double extra strong
   D. type M copper

39.____

40. Assume that a shop is undergoing a general housecleaning, and all excess unused materials have been removed. *Clean-up work,* as pertains to painting in this case, means MOST NEARLY

   A. a thorough two-coat paint job
   B. only that surface which was marred to be painted
   C. a one-coat job to *freshen things up*
   D. only that iron work is to be painted

40.____

41. The *United States Standard Gage* is used to measure sheet metal thicknesses of

   A. iron and steel
   B. aluminum
   C. copper
   D. tin

41.____

42. Headers and stretchers are used in the construction of

   A. floors   B. walls   C. ceilings   D. roofs

42.____

Questions 43-44.

DIRECTIONS: Questions 43 and 44, inclusive, are to be answered in accordance with the following paragraph.

For cast iron pipe lines, the middle ring or sleeve shall have <u>beveled</u> ends and shall be high quality cast iron. The middle ring shall have a minimum wall thickness of 3/8" for pipe up to 8", 7/16" for pipe 10" to 30", and 1/2" for pipe over 30", nominal diameter. Minimum length of middle ring shall be 5" for pipe up to 10", 6" for pipe 10" to 30", and 10" for pipe 30" nominal diameter and larger. The middle ring shall not have a center pipe stop, unless otherwise specified.

43. As used in the above paragraph, the word *beveled* means MOST NEARLY

   A. straight   B. slanted   C. curved   D. rounded

43.____

44. In accordance with the above paragraph, the middle ring of a 24" nominal diameter pipe would have a minimum wall thickness and length of _____ thick and _____ long.

   A. 3/8"; 5"   B. 3/8"; 6"   C. 7/16"; 6"   D. 1/2"; 6"

44.____

45. A work order is NOT usually issued for which one of the following jobs:

    A. Repairing wood door frames
    B. Taking daily inventory
    C. Installing electric switches in maintenance shop
    D. Repairing a number of valves in boiler room

46. Of the following statements, the one which usually does NOT pertain to preventative maintenance programs is

    A. periodic inspection of facilities
    B. lubrication of equipment
    C. minor repair of equipment
    D. complete replacement of deteriorated equipment

Questions 47-50.

DIRECTIONS: Questions 47 through 50, inclusive, are based on the sketch of metal sheet shown below. (Sketch not to scale.)

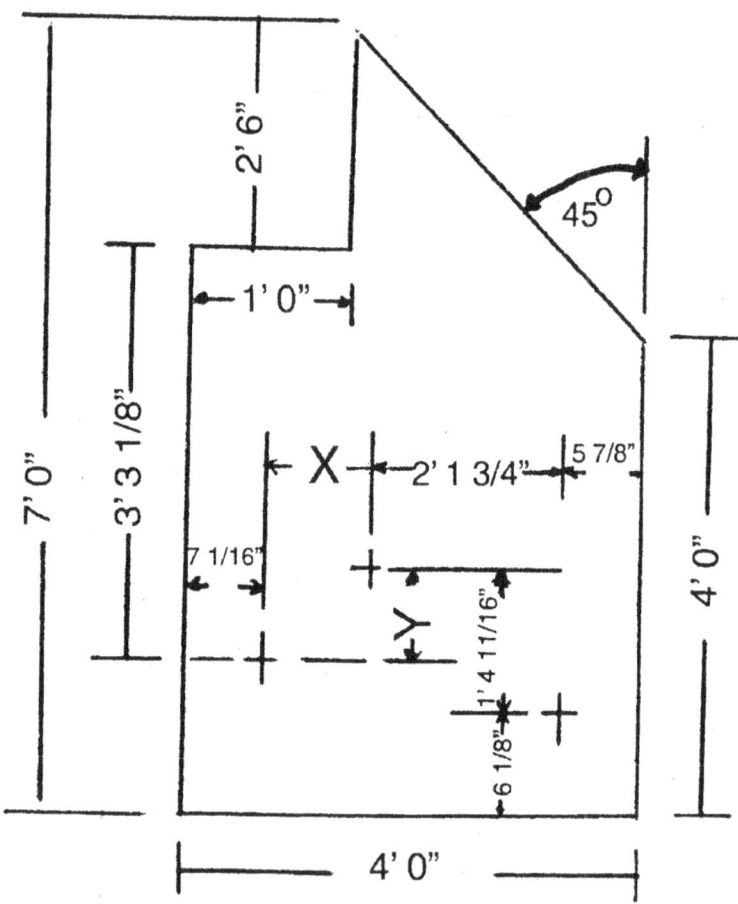

47. From the above sketch, the distance marked X is MOST NEARLY

    A. 5 1/4"   B. 6 5/16"   C. 7 1/8"   D. 9 5/16"

48. From the above sketch, the distance marked Y is MOST NEARLY 48.____

   A. 5 11/16"   B. 6 3/16"   C. 7 5/16"   D. 8 11/16"

49. In reference to the above sketch, if each piece is made from a rectangular piece of metal measuring 4' x 7', the percent of waste material is MOST NEARLY 49.____

   A. 10%   B. 15%   C. 25%   D. 30%

50. In reference to the above sketch, if the metal is 1/4" thick and weighs 144 pounds per cubic foot, the net weight of one piece would be MOST NEARLY _____ pounds. 50.____

   A. 51   B. 63   C. 75   D. 749

KEY (CORRECT ANSWERS)

1. C	11. A	21. B	31. A	41. A
2. D	12. C	22. C	32. A	42. B
3. A	13. A	23. D	33. A	43. B
4. D	14. D	24. B	34. D	44. C
5. C	15. B	25. D	35. C	45. B
6. B	16. A	26. D	36. B	46. D
7. C	17. C	27. A	37. D	47. D
8. C	18. C	28. C	38. B	48. D
9. D	19. B	29. D	39. A	49. C
10. A	20. B	30. D	40. C	50. B

EXAMINATION SECTION
TEST 1

DIRECTIONS: Each question or incomplete statement is followed by several suggested answers or completions. Select the one that BEST answers the question or completes the statement. *PRINT THE LETTER OF THE CORRECT ANSWER IN THE SPACE AT THE RIGHT.*

1. A maintenance man complains to you that he is getting all the boring jobs to do. You check and find that his complaint has no basis in fact.
The one of the following which is the MOST likely reason why the maintenance man made such a claim is that he

   A. wants to get even with the supervisor
   B. lives in a world of fantasy
   C. believes the injustice to be real
   D. is jealous of other workers

   1.____

2. When on preliminary review of a mechanic's written grievance you feel the grievance to be unfounded, the FIRST step you should take is to

   A. show the mechanic where he is wrong
   B. check carefully to find out why the mechanic thinks that way
   C. try to humor the mechanic out of it
   D. tell the mechanic to stop complaining

   2.____

3. Assume that you decide to hold a private meeting with one of your mechanics who has a drinking problem that is affecting his work.
At the meeting, the BEST way for you to handle this situation is to

   A. tell the mechanic off and then listen to what he has to say
   B. criticize the mechanic's behavior to get him to *open up* in order to help him correct his problem quickly
   C. try to get the mechanic to recognize his problem and find ways to solve it
   D. limit the discussion to matters concerning only the problem and look for immediate results

   3.____

4. The one of the following which is a generally accepted guide in criticizing a subordinate EFFECTIVELY is to

   A. criticize the improper act, not the individual
   B. put the listener on the defensive
   C. make the criticism general instead of specific
   D. correct the personality, not the situation

   4.____

5. The one of the following disciplinary methods by which you are MOST likely to be successful in getting a problem employee to improve his behavior is when you

   A. discipline the employee in front of others
   B. consider the matter to be ended after the disciplining
   C. give the exact same discipline no matter how serious the wrongdoing
   D. make an example of the employee

   5.____

6. Of the following statements, the one that is MOST applicable to a disciplinary situation is that discipline should be

   A. used after a cooling-off period
   B. identical for all employees
   C. consistent with the violation
   D. based on personal feelings

7. The one of the following approaches that is MOST important for you to take in evaluating a mechanic in order to increase his work productivity is to

   A. first have him evaluate his own performance
   B. meet with him to discuss how he is doing and what is expected on the job
   C. send him a copy of your evaluation of his work performance and give him the opportunity to submit written comments
   D. express in writing your appreciation of his work

8. Assume that you say to one of the mechanics, *Jim, that job you turned out today was top-notch. I didn't think you could do so well with the kind of material you had to work with.*
   This statement BEST describes an example of your

   A. recognition of the man's work
   B. disrespect for the man's feelings
   C. personal favoritism of the man
   D. constructive criticism of the man's work

9. In general, the OUTSTANDING characteristic of employees over 50 years of age is their

   A. resistance   B. endurance
   C. wisdom   D. job stability

10. You should be interested in the morale of your men because morale is MOST often associated with

    A. mechanization   B. automation
    C. production   D. seniority regulations

11. Assume that the maintenance work order system is about to be changed. Your workers would MOST likely show the LEAST resistance to this change if you

    A. downgrade the old maintenance work order system
    B. tell your workers how the change will benefit them
    C. post the notice of the change on the bulletin board
    D. tell the workers how the change will benefit management

12. Of the following, the BEST way to motivate a newly appointed mechanic is to

    A. explain the meaning of each assignment
    B. make the work more physically demanding
    C. test the mechanic's ability
    D. use as much authority as possible

13. The one of the following which is the LEAST important reason for giving employees information concerning policy changes which will affect them is that employees should know

    A. why the change is being made
    B. who will be affected by the change
    C. when the change will go into effect
    D. how much savings will be made by the change

14. A foreman who knows how to handle his men will MOST likely get them to produce more by treating them

    A. alike
    B. as individuals
    C. on a casual basis
    D. as a group

15. Of the following items, the one that a supervisor has the MOST right to expect from his employees is

    A. liking the job
    B. a fair day's work
    C. equal skill of all mechanics
    D. perfection

16. The one of the following which is the BEST practice for you to follow in handling a dispute between the workers is to

    A. side with one of the workers so as to end the dispute quickly
    B. pay no attention to the dispute and let the workers settle it themselves
    C. listen to each worker's story of the dispute and then decide how to settle it
    D. discuss the dispute with other workers and then decide how to settle it

17. You are likely to run into an employee morale problem when assigning a dirty job that comes up often.
    Of the following, the BEST method of assigning this work is to

    A. rotate this assignment
    B. assign it to the fastest worker
    C. assign it by seniority
    D. assign it to the least skilled worker

18. Of the following, the one that is generally regarded as the BEST aid to high work productivity of subordinates is a supervisor's skill in

    A. record keeping
    B. technical work
    C. setting up rules and regulations
    D. human relations

19. The BEST way to help a mechanic who comes to you for advice on a personal problem is to

    A. listen to the worker's problem without passing judgment
    B. tell the worker to forget about the problem and to stop letting it interfere with his work
    C. talk about your own personal problems to the worker
    D. mind your own business and leave the worker alone

4 (#1)

20. You are in charge of the maintenance shop and have learned that within the next two weeks the maintenance shop will be moved to a new location on the plant grounds, but you have not learned why this move is taking place. Assume that you have decided not to keep this information from your mechanics until the reason is known but to inform them of this matter now.
Of the following, which one is the BEST argument that can be made regarding your decision?

   A. *Acceptable;* because although the reason is not now known, the mechanics will eventually find out about the move
   B. *Unacceptable;* because the mechanics do not know at this time the reason for the move and this will cause anxiety on their part
   C. *Acceptable*; because the mechanics will be affected by the move and they should be told what is happening
   D. *Unacceptable;* because the mechanics' advance knowledge of the move will tend to slow down their work output

21. Of the following, the FIRST action for a foreman to take in making a decision is to

   A. get all the facts
   B. develop alternate solutions
   C. get opinions of others
   D. know the results in advance

22. Assume that you have just been promoted to foreman.
Of the following, the BEST practice to follow regarding your previous experience at the mechanic's level is to

   A. continue to fraternize with your old friends
   B. use this experience to better understand those who now work for you
   C. use your old connections to keep top management informed of mechanics' views
   D. forget the mechanics' points of view

23. You have decided to hold regular group discussions with your subordinates on various aspects of their duties.
Of the following methods you might use to begin such a program, the one which is likely to be MOST productive is to

   A. express your own ideas and persuade the group to accept them
   B. save time and cover more ground by asking questions calling for yes or no answers
   C. propose to the group a general plan of action rather than specific ideas carefully worked out
   D. provide an informal atmosphere for the exchange of ideas

24. The principle of learning by which a foreman might get the BEST results in training his subordinates is:

   A. Letting the learner discover and correct his own mistakes
   B. Teaching the most technical part of the work first
   C. Teaching all parts of the work during the first training session
   D. Getting the learner to use as many of his five senses as possible

25. A new mechanic is to be trained to do an involved operation containing several steps of varying difficulty. This mechanic will MOST likely learn the operation more quickly if he is taught

 A. each step in its proper order
 B. the hardest steps first
 C. the easiest steps first
 D. first the steps that do not require tools

25.____

KEY (CORRECT ANSWERS)

1.	C	11.	B
2.	B	12.	A
3.	C	13.	D
4.	A	14.	B
5.	B	15.	B
6.	C	16.	C
7.	B	17.	A
8.	A	18.	D
9.	D	19.	A
10.	C	20.	C

21.	A
22.	B
23.	D
24.	D
25.	C

TEST 2

DIRECTIONS: Each question or incomplete statement is followed by several suggested answers or completions. Select the one that BEST answers the question or completes the statement. *PRINT THE LETTER OF THE CORRECT ANSWER IN THE SPACE AT THE RIGHT.*

1. The one of the following job situations in which it is better to give a written order than an oral order is when

    A. the job involves many details
    B. you can check the job's progress easily
    C. the job is repetitive in nature
    D. there is an emergency

2. Which one of the following serves as the BEST guideline for you to follow for effective written reports?
    Keep sentences

    A. short and limit sentences to one thought
    B. short and use as many thoughts as possible
    C. long and limit sentences to one thought
    D. long and use as many thoughts as possible

3. Of the following, the BEST reason why a foreman generally should not do the work of an individual mechanic is that

    A. the shop's production figures will not be accurate
    B. a foreman is paid to supervise
    C. the foreman must maintain his authority
    D. the employee may become self-conscious

4. One method by which a foreman might prepare written reports to management is to begin with the conclusions, results, or summary and to follow this with the supporting data.
    The BEST reason why management may prefer this form of report is because

    A. management lacks the specific training to understand the data
    B. the data completely supports the conclusions
    C. time is saved by getting to the conclusions of the report first
    D. the data contains all the information that is required for making the conclusions

5. Forms used for time records and work orders are important to the work of a foreman PRIMARILY because they give him

    A. the knowledge of and familiarity with work operations
    B. the means of control of personnel, material, or job costs
    C. the means for communicating with other workers
    D. a useful method for making filing procedures easier

6. The one of the following which is the MOST important factor in determining the number of employees you can effectively supervise is the

   A. type of work to be performed
   B. priority of the work to be performed
   C. salary level of the workers
   D. ratio of permanent employees to temporary employees

6.____

7. Of the following, you will be MOST productive in carrying out your supervisory responsibilities if you

   A. are capable of doing the same work as your mechanics
   B. meet with your mechanics frequently
   C. are very friendly with your mechanics
   D. get work done through your mechanics

7.____

8. You have been asked to prepare the annual budget for your maintenance shop.
   The one of the following which is the FIRST step you should take in preparing this budget is to determine the

   A. amount of maintenance work which is scheduled for the shop
   B. time it takes for a specific unit of work to be completed
   C. current workload of each employee in the shop
   D. policies and procedures of the shop's operations

8.____

9. When determining the amount of work you expect a group of mechanics to perform in a given time, the BEST procedure for you to follow should be to

   A. aim for a higher level of production than that of the most productive worker
   B. stay at the present production level
   C. set general instead of specific goals
   D. let workers participate in the determination whenever possible

9.____

10. You have been asked to set next year's performance goals concerning the ratio of jobs completed on schedule to total jobs worked. A review of last year's record shows that the workers completed their jobs on schedule 85% of the time, with the best ones showing an on-time ratio of 92% and the poorest ones showing an on-time ratio of 65%.
    Using these facts in line with generally accepted goal-setting practices, you should set a performance ratio for the next year on the basis of _____ average with a _____ minimum acceptable for any employee.

    A. 85%; 65%   B. 85%; 70%   C. 90%; 65%   D. 90%; 70%

10.____

11. It is important for you to be able to identify the critical parts of a large project such as the remodeling of your maintenance shop.
    The one of the following which is the BEST reason why this is important is that it may

    A. help you to set up good communications between you and your workers
    B. give you a better understanding of the purpose of the project
    C. give you control over the time and cost involved in the project
    D. help you to determine who are your most productive workers

11.____

12. When doing work planning for your shop, the factor that you should normally consider LAST among the following is knowing your

    A. major objectives
    B. record keeping system
    C. minor objectives
    D. priorities

13. You have the responsibility for ordering all materials for your maintenance shop. A listing of materials needed for the operations of your shop is long overdue. You realize that you are unable to find time to take care of the inventory personally because of a high priority project you have been working on which has been taking all of your time. You do not know when you will be finished with the project.
    The BEST of the following courses of action to take in handling this inventory matter is to

    A. request that you be taken off the project immediately so that you may take care of the inventory
    B. complete your high priority project and then do the inventory yourself
    C. volunteer to work overtime so that you may complete the inventory while continuing with the project
    D. assign the inventory work to a competent subordinate

14. You have the authority and responsibility for seeing that proper records are kept in your shop. Assume that you decide to delegate to a records clerk the responsibility for collecting the time sheets and the authority to make changes on the time sheets to correct the information when necessary.
    Of the following, which one is the BEST argument that can be made regarding your decision?

    A. *Unacceptable*; because you can delegate only your responsibility but none of your authority to the records clerk
    B. *Acceptable*; because you can delegate some of your authority and some of your responsibility to the records clerk
    C. *Unacceptable;* because you can delegate only your authority but none of your responsibility to the records clerk
    D. *Acceptable;* because you can delegate all your responsibility and all your authority to the records clerk

15. You will LEAST likely be able to do an effective job of controlling operating costs if you

    A. eliminate idle time
    B. reduce absenteeism
    C. raise your budget
    D. combine work operations

16. Of the following actions, the one which is LEAST likely to help in carrying out your responsibilities of looking after the interests of your workers is to

    A. crack down on your workers when necessary
    B. let your workers know that you support company policy
    C. prevent the transfers of your workers
    D. back up your workers in a controversy

17. The term *accountability*, as used in management of supervision, means MOST NEARLY

    A. responsibility for results
    B. record keeping
    C. bookkeeping systems
    D. inventory control

18. Assume that you have been unable to convince an employee of the seriousness of his poor attendance record by talking to him.
The one of the following which is the BEST course of action for you to take is to

    A. keep talking to the employee
    B. recommend that a written warning be given
    C. consider transferring the employee to another work location
    D. recommend that the employee be fired

19. When delegating work to a subordinate foreman, you should NOT

    A. delegate the right to make any decisions
    B. be interested in the results of the work, but in the method of doing the work
    C. delegate any work that you can do better than your subordinate
    D. give up your final responsibility for the work

20. Of the following statements, the BEST reason why proper scheduling of maintenance work is important is that it

    A. eliminates the need for individual job work orders
    B. classifies job skills in accordance with performance
    C. minimizes lost time in performing any maintenance job
    D. determines needed repairs in various locations

21. Of the following factors, the one which is of LEAST importance in determining the number of subordinates that an individual should be assigned to supervise is the

    A. nature of the work being supervised
    B. qualifications of the individual as a supervisor
    C. capabilities of the subordinates
    D. lines of promotion for the subordinates

22. Suppose that a large number of semi-literate residents of this city have been requesting the assistance of your department. You are asked to prepare a form which these applicants will be required to fill out before their requests will be considered.
In view of these facts, the one of the following factors to which you should give the GREATEST amount of consideration in preparing this form is the

    A. size of the form
    B. sequence of the information asked for on the form
    C. level of difficulty of the language used in the form
    D. number of times which the form will have to be reviewed

23. A budget is a plan whereby a goal is set for future operations. It affords a medium for comparing actual expenditures with planned expenditures.
The one of the following which is the MOST accurate statement on the basis of this statement is that

    A. the budget serves as an accurate measure of past as well as future expenditures
    B. the budget presents an estimate of expenditures to be made in the future
    C. budget estimates should be based upon past budget requirements
    D. planned expenditures usually fall short of actual expenditures

24. A foreman who is familiar with modern management principles should know that the one of the following requirements of an administrator which is LEAST important is his ability to

   A. coordinate work
   B. plan, organize, and direct the work under his control
   C. cooperate with others
   D. perform the duties of the employees under his jurisdiction

25. The one of the following which should be considered the LEAST important objective of the service rating system is to

   A. rate the employees on the basis of their potential abilities
   B. establish a basis for assigning employees to special types of work
   C. provide a means of recognizing superior work performance
   D. reveal the need for training as well as the effectiveness of a training program

KEY (CORRECT ANSWERS)

1. A		11. C	
2. A		12. B	
3. B		13. D	
4. C		14. B	
5. B		15. C	
6. A		16. C	
7. D		17. A	
8. A		18. B	
9. D		19. D	
10. D		20. C	

21. D
22. C
23. B
24. D
25. A

EXAMINATION SECTION
TEST 1

DIRECTIONS: Each question or incomplete statement is followed by several suggested answers or completions. Select the one that BEST answers the question or completes the statement. *PRINT THE LETTER OF THE CORRECT ANSWER IN THE SPACE AT THE RIGHT.*

1. Of the following, the one MOST important quality required of a good supervisor is
    A. ambition   B. leadership   C. friendliness   D. popularity

2. It is often said that a supervisor can delegate authority but never responsibility. This means MOST NEARLY that
    A. a supervisor must do his own work if he expects it to be done properly
    B. a supervisor can assign someone else to do his work, but in the last analysis, the supervisor himself must take the blame for any actions followed
    C. authority and responsibility are two separate things that cannot be borne by the same person
    D. it is better for a supervisor never to delegate his authority

3. One of your men who is a habitual complainer asks you to grant him a minor privilege.
Before granting or denying such a request, you should consider
    A. the merits of the case
    B. that it is good for group morale to grant a request of this nature
    C. the man's seniority
    D. that to deny such a request will lower your standing with the men

4. A supervisory practice on the part of a foreman which is MOST likely to lead to confusion and inefficiency is for him to
    A. give orders verbally directly to the man assigned to the job
    B. issue orders only in writing
    C. follow up his orders after issuing them
    D. relay his orders to the men through co-workers

5. It would be POOR supervision on a foreman's part if he
    A. asked an experienced maintainer for his opinion on the method of doing a special job
    B. make it a policy to avoid criticizing a man in front of his co-workers
    C. consulted his assistant supervisor on unusual problems
    D. allowed a cooling-off period of several days before giving one of his men a deserved reprimand

6. Of the following behavior characteristics of a supervisor, the one that is MOST likely to lower the morale of the men he supervises is
   A. diligence
   B. favoritism
   C. punctuality
   D. thoroughness

7. Of the following, the BEST method of getting an employee who is not working up to his capacity to produce more work is to
   A. have another employee criticize his production
   B. privately criticize his production but encourage him to produce more
   C. criticize his production before his associates
   D. criticize his production and threaten to fire him

8. Of the following, the BEST thing for a supervisor to do when a subordinate has done a very good job is to
   A. tell him to take it easy
   B. praise his work
   C. reduce his workload
   D. say nothing because he may become conceited

9. Your orders to your crew are MOST likely to be followed if you
   A. explain the reasons for these orders
   B. warn that all violators will be punished
   C. promise easy assignments to those who follow these orders best
   D. say that they are for the good of the department

10. In order to be a good supervisor, you should
    A. impress upon your men that you demand perfection in their work at all times
    B. avoid being blamed for your crew's mistakes
    C. impress your superior with your ability
    D. see to it that your men get what they are entitled to

11. In giving instructions to a crew, you should
    A. speak in as loud a tone as possible
    B. speak in a coaxing, persuasive manner
    C. speak quietly, clearly, and courteously
    D. always use the word *please* when giving instructions

12. Of the following factors, the one which is LEAST important in evaluating an employee and his work is his
    A. dependability
    B. quantity of work done
    C. quality of work done
    D. education and training

13. When a District Superintendent first assumes his command, it is LEAST important for him at the beginning to observe
    A. how his equipment is designed and its adaptability
    B. how to reorganize the district for greater efficiency
    C. the capabilities of the men in the district
    D. the methods of operation being employed

14. When making an inspection of one of the buildings under your supervision, the BEST procedure to follow in making a record of the inspection is to
    A. return immediately to the office and write a report from memory
    B. write down all the important facts during or as soon as you complete the inspection
    C. fix in your mind all important facts so that you can repeat them from memory if necessary
    D. fix in your mind all important facts so that you can make out your report at the end of the day

15. Assume that your superior has directed you to make certain changes in your established procedure. After using this modified procedure on several occasions, you find that the original procedure was distinctly superior and you wish to return to it.
    You should
    A. let your superior find this out for himself
    B. simply change back to the original procedure
    C. compile definite data and information to prove your case to your superior
    D. persuade one of the more experienced workers to take this matter up with your superior

16. An inspector visited a large building under construction. He inspected the soil lines at 9 A.M., water lines at 10 A.M., fixtures at 11 A.M., and did his office work in the afternoon. He followed the same pattern daily for weeks.
    This procedure was
    A. *good*, because it was methodical and he did not miss anything
    B. *good*, because it gave equal time to all phases of the plumbing
    C. *bad*, because not enough time was devoted to fixtures
    D. *bad*, because the tradesmen knew when the inspection would occur

17. Assume that one of the foremen in a training course, which you are conducting, proposes a poor solution for a maintenance problem.
    Of the following, the BEST course of action for you to take is to
    A. accept the solution tentatively and correct it during the next class meeting
    B. point out all the defects of this proposed solution and wait until somebody thinks of a better solution
    C. try to get the class to reject this proposed solution and develop a better solution
    D. let the matter pass since somebody will present a better solution as the class work proceeds

18. As a supervisor, you should be seeking ways to improve the efficiency of shop operations by means such as changing established work procedures.
    The following are offered as possible actions that you should consider in changing established work procedures:
    I. Make changes only when your foremen agree to them
    II. Discuss changes with your supervisor before putting them into practice

4 (#1)

III. Standardize any operation which is performed on a continuing basis
IV. Make changes quickly and quietly in order to avoid dissent
V. Secure expert guidance before instituting unfamiliar procedures
Of the following suggested answers, the one that describes the actions to be taken to change established work procedures is
    A. I, IV, V   B. II, III, V   C. III, IV, V   D. All of the above

19. A supervisor determined that a foreman, without informing his superior, delegated responsibility for checking time cards to a member of his gang. The supervisor then called the foreman into his office where he reprimanded the foreman.
    This action of the supervisor in reprimanding the foreman was
    A. *proper*, because the checking of time cards is the foreman's responsibility and should not be delegated
    B. *proper*, because the foreman did not ask the supervisor for permission to delegate responsibility
    C. *improper*, because the foreman may no longer take the initiative in solving future problems
    D. *improper*, because the supervisor is interfering in a function which is not his responsibility

19.____

20. A capable supervisor should check all operations under his control.
    Of the following, the LEAST important reason for doing this is to make sure that
    A. operations are being performed as scheduled
    B. he personally observes all operations at all times
    C. all the operations are still needed
    D. his manpower is being utilized efficiently

20.____

21. A supervisor makes it a practice to apply fair and firm discipline in all cases of rule infractions, including those of a minor nature.
    This practice should PRIMARILY be considered
    A. *bad*, since applying discipline for minor violations is a waste of time
    B. *good*, because not applying discipline for minor infractions can lead to a more serious erosion of discipline
    C. *bad*, because employees do not like to be disciplined for minor violations of the rules
    D. *good*, because violating any rule can cause a dangerous situation to occur

21.____

22. A maintainer would PROPERLY consider it poor supervisory practice for a foreman to consult with him on
    A. which of several repair jobs should be scheduled first
    B. how to cope with personal problems at home
    C. whether the neatness of his headquarters can be improved
    D. how to express a suggestion which the maintainer plans to submit formally

22.____

23. Assume that you have determined that the work of one of your foremen and the men he supervises is consistently behind schedule. When you discuss this situation with the foreman, he tells you that his men are poor workers and then complains that he must spend all of his time checking on their work.
The following actions are offered for your consideration as possible ways of solving the problem of poor performance of the foreman and his men:
   I. Review the work standards with the foreman and determine whether they are realistic.
   II. Tell the foreman that you will recommend him for the foreman's training course for retraining.
   III. Ask the foreman for the names of the maintainers and then replace them as soon as possible.
   IV. Tell the foreman that you expect him to meet a satisfactory level of performance.
   V. Tell the foreman to insist that his men work overtime to catch up to the schedule.
   VI. Tell the foreman to review the type and amount of training he has given the maintainers.
   VII. Tell the foreman that he will be out of a job if he does not produce on schedule.
   VIII. Avoid all criticism of the foreman and his methods.
Which of the following suggested answers CORRECTLY lists the proper actions to be taken to solve the problem of poor performance of the foreman and his men?
   A. I, II, IV, VI   B. I, III, V, VII   C. II, III, VI, VIII   D. IV, V, VI, VIII

24. When a conference or a group discussion is tending to turn into a *bull session* without constructive purpose, the BEST action to take is to
   A. reprimand the leader of the bull session
   B. redirect the discussion to the business at hand
   C. dismiss the meeting and reschedule it for another day
   D. allow the bull session to continue

25. Assume that you have been assigned responsibility for a program in which a high production rate is mandatory. From past experience, you know that your foremen do not perform equally well in the various types of jobs given to them. Which of the following methods should you use in selecting foremen for the specific types of work involved in the program?
   A. Leave the method of selecting foremen to your supervisor
   B. Assign each foreman to the work he does best
   C. Allow each foreman to choose his own job
   D. Assign each foreman to a job which will permit him to improve his own abilities

KEY (CORRECT ANSWERS)

1.	B	11.	C
2.	B	12.	D
3.	A	13.	B
4.	D	14.	B
5.	D	15.	C
6.	B	16.	D
7.	B	17.	C
8.	B	18.	B
9.	A	19.	A
10.	D	20.	B

21. B
22. A
23. A
24. B
25. B

TEST 2

DIRECTIONS: Each question or incomplete statement is followed by several suggested answers or completions. Select the one that BEST answers the question or completes the statement. *PRINT THE LETTER OF THE CORRECT ANSWER IN THE SPACE AT THE RIGHT.*

1. A foreman who is familiar with modern management principles should know that the one of the following requirements of an administrator which is LEAST important is his ability to
   A. coordinate work
   B. plan, organize, and direct the work under his control
   C. cooperate with others
   D. perform the duties of the employees under his jurisdiction

2. When subordinates request his advice in solving problems encountered in their work, a certain chief occasionally answers the request by first asking the subordinate what he thinks should be done.
   This action by the chief is, on the whole,
   A. *desirable*, because it stimulates subordinates to give more thought to the solution of problems encountered
   B. *undesirable*, because it discourages subordinates from asking questions
   C. *desirable*, because it discourages subordinates from asking questions
   D. *undesirable*, because it undermines the confidence of subordinates in the ability of their supervisor

3. Of the following factors that may be considered by a unit head in dealing with the tardy subordinate, the one which should be given LEAST consideration is the
   A. frequency with which the employee is tardy
   B. effect of the employee's tardiness upon the work of other employees
   C. willingness of the employee to work overtime when necessary
   D. cause of the employee's tardiness

4. The MOST important requirement of a good inspectional report is that it should be
   A. properly addressed
   B. lengthy
   C. clear and brief
   D. spelled correctly

5. Building superintendents frequently inquire about departmental inspectional procedures.
   Of the following, it is BEST to
   A. advise them to write to the department for an official reply
   B. refuse as the inspectional procedure is a restricted matter
   C. briefly explain the procedure to them
   D. avoid the inquiry by changing the subject

6. Reprimanding a crew member before other workers is a
    A. *good* practice; the reprimand serves as a warning to the other workers
    B. *bad* practice; people usually resent criticism made in public
    C. *good* practice; the other workers will realize that the supervisor is fair
    D. *bad* practice; the other workers will take sides in the dispute

7. Of the following actions, the one which is LEAST likely to promote good work is for the group leader to
    A. praise workers for doing a good job
    B. call attention to the opportunities for promotion for better workers
    C. threaten to recommend discharge of workers who are below standard
    D. put into practice any good suggestion made by crew members

8. A supervisor notices that a member of his crew has skipped a routine step in his job.
   Of the following, the BEST action for the supervisor to take is to
    A. promptly question the worker about the incident
    B. immediately assign another man to complete the job
    C. bring up the incident the next time the worker asks for a favor
    D. say nothing about the incident but watch the worker carefully in the future

9. Assume you have been told to show a new worker how to operate a piece of equipment.
   Your FIRST step should be to
    A. ask the worker if he has any questions about the equipment
    B. permit the worker to operate the equipment himself while you carefully watch to prevent damage
    C. demonstrate the operation of the equipment for the worker
    D. have the worker read an instruction booklet on the maintenance of the equipment

10. Whenever a new man was assigned to his crew, the supervisor would introduce him to all other crew members, take him on a tour of the plant, tell him about bus schedules and places to eat.
    This practice is
    A. *good*; the new man is made to feel welcome
    B. *bad*; supervisors should not interfere in personal matters
    C. *good*; the new man knows that he can bring his personal problems to the supervisor
    D. *bad*; work time should not be spent on personal matters

11. The MOST important factor in successful leadership is the ability to
    A. obtain instant obedience to all orders
    B. establish friendly personal relations with crew members
    C. avoid disciplining crew members
    D. make crew members want to do what should be done

12. Explaining the reasons for departmental procedure to workers tends to
    A. waste time which should be used for productive purposes
    B. increase their interest in their work
    C. make them more critical of departmental procedures
    D. confuse them

13. If you want a job done well do it yourself.
    For a supervisor to follow this advice would be
    A. *good*; a supervisor is responsible for the work of his crew
    B. *bad*; a supervisor should train his men, not do their work
    C. *good*; a supervisor should be skilled in all jobs assigned to his crew
    D. *bad*; a supervisor loses respect when he works with his hands

14. When a supervisor discovers a mistake in one of the jobs for which his crew is responsible, it is MOST important for him to find out
    A. whether anybody else knows about the mistake
    B. who was to blame for the mistake
    C. how to prevent similar mistakes in the future
    D. whether similar mistakes occurred in the past

15. A supervisor who has to explain a new procedure to his crew should realize that questions from the crew USUALLY show that they
    A. are opposed to the new practice
    B. are completely confused by the explanation
    C. need more training in the new procedure
    D. are interested in the explanation

16. A good way for a supervisor to retain the confidence of his or her employees is to
    A. say as little as possible
    B. check work frequently
    C. make no promises unless they will be fulfilled
    D. never hesitate in giving an answer to any question

17. Good supervision is ESSENTIALLY a matter of
    A. patience in supervising workers   B. care in selecting workers
    C. skill in human relations   D. fairness in disciplining workers

18. It is MOST important for an employee who has been assigned a monotonous task to
    A. perform this task before doing other work
    B. ask another employee to help
    C. perform this task only after all other work has been completed
    D. take measures to prevent mistakes in performing the task

19. One of your employees has violated a minor agency regulation.
    The FIRST thing you should do is
    A. warn the employee that you will have to take disciplinary action if it should happen again
    B. ask the employee to explain his or her actions
    C. inform your supervisor and wait for advice
    D. write a memo describing the incident and place it in the employee's personnel file

19.____

20. One of your employees tells you that he feels you give him much more work than the other employees, and he is having trouble meeting your deadlines.
    You should
    A. ask if he has been under a lot of non-work related stress lately
    B. review his recent assignments to determine if he is correct
    C. explain that this is a busy time, but you are dividing the work equally
    D. tell him that he is the most competent employee and that is why he receives more work

20.____

21. A supervisor assigns one of his crew to complete a portion of a job. A short time later, the supervisor notices that the portion has not been completed.
    Of the following, the BEST way for the supervisor to handle this is to
    A. ask the crew member why he has not completed the assignment
    B. reprimand the crew member for not obeying orders
    C. assign another crew member to complete the assignment
    D. complete the assignment himself

21.____

22. Supposes that a member of your crew complains that you are *playing favorites* in assigning work.
    Of the following, the BEST method of handling the complaint is to
    A. deny it and refuse to discuss the matter with the worker
    B. take the opportunity to tell the worker what is wrong with his work
    C. ask the worker for examples to prove his point and try to clear up any misunderstanding
    D. promise to be more careful in making assignments in the future

22.____

23. A member of your crew comes to you with a complaint. After discussing the matter with him, it is clear that you have convinced him that his complaint was not justified.
    At this point, you should
    A. permit him to drop the matter
    B. make him admit his error
    C. pretend to see some justification in his complaint
    D. warn him against making unjustified complaints

23.____

24. Suppose that a supervisor has in his crew an older man who works rather slowly. In other respects, this man is a good worker; he is seldom absent, works carefully, never loafs, and is cooperative.

24.____

The BEST way for the supervisor to handle this worker is to
   A. try to get him to work faster and less carefully
   B. give him the most disagreeable job
   C. request that he be given special training
   D. permit him to work at his own speed

25. Suppose that a member of your crew comes to you with a suggestion he thinks will save time in doing a job. You realize immediately that it won't work. Under these circumstances, your BEST action would be to
   A. thank the worker for the suggestion and forget about it
   B. explain to the worker why you think it won't work
   C. tell the worker to put the suggestion in writing
   D. ask the other members of your crew to criticize the suggestion

25.____

KEY (CORRECT ANSWERS)

1.	D	11.	D
2.	A	12.	B
3.	C	13.	B
4.	C	14.	C
5.	C	15.	D
6.	B	16.	C
7.	C	17.	C
8.	A	18.	D
9.	C	19.	B
10.	A	20.	B

21.	A
22.	C
23.	A
24.	D
25.	B

EXAMINATION SECTION
TEST 1

DIRECTIONS: Each question or incomplete statement is followed by several suggested answers or completions. Select the one that BEST answers the question or completes the statement. *PRINT THE LETTER OF THE CORRECT ANSWER IN THE SPACE AT THE RIGHT.*

1. The BEST course of action to take to settle a job-related dispute that has arisen among two of your employees is to

    A. bring them both together, listen to their arguments, and then make a decision
    B. tell the two employees individually to settle their dispute
    C. tell both employees to submit their dispute in writing to you and then make a decision
    D. listen to the argument of each one separately and then make a decision

2. A custodian accidentally discovers a bottle of whiskey in a staff member's desk. The BEST procedure for the custodian to follow is to

    A. verbally reprimand him and prefer departmental charges
    B. inform him that whiskey is not allowed in school buildings
    C. call a meeting of all the employees and tell them what you found
    D. do nothing as you do not want to embarrass the person

3. A new employee under your supervision constantly reports late for work. The one of the following actions you should take FIRST is to

    A. admonish him in front of the other employees
    B. prefer charges against him
    C. transfer him to another school
    D. warn him that he must be on time

4. The one of the following procedures that is BEST to follow when it is necessary to reprimand a worker is to

    A. issue the same reprimand to all your men
    B. avoid him so he won't feel bad
    C. speak to him privately about the matter
    D. tell him what he has done wrong immediately to teach the other employees a lesson

5. The LEAST important factor to consider when evaluating the work of an employee is

    A. his grade on his civil service test
    B. the quality of his work
    C. his resourcefulness
    D. his attendance record

6. The one of the following supervisory actions that a custodian should use LEAST often is to 6.___

   A. make periodic reports to his superior about the work of his men
   B. bring employees up on "charges" whenever they do anything wrong
   C. listen to staff grievances
   D. advise an employee concerning a personal problem

7. The MAIN supervisory responsibility of a custodian is to 7.___

   A. foster policies of the board and the parents' organizations
   B. do his job so well that the students and employees like him
   C. make assignments to his employees
   D. keep the building and grounds in good operating condition

8. One of your employees verbally protests to you about your evaluation of his work. The BEST way to handle him is to 8.___

   A. advise him of your lengthy and qualified experience
   B. tell him that you do not care to talk about it
   C. explain to him how you arrived at your evaluation
   D. tell him that since all the other employees are satisfied, he should withdraw his complaint

9. A custodian will BEST keep the morale of his men high by 9.___

   A. giving praise for well-done work
   B. assigning good workers the most work
   C. personally helping each man in all the details of the man's job
   D. allowing special privileges for good work

10. In training maintenance personnel under the supervision of a custodian, the one of the following that should be given LEAST consideration by the custodian is 10.___

    A. how the training is to be given
    B. who is to be trained
    C. when the training will be given
    D. how the school principal wants them to be trained

11. The BEST attitude for a custodian to follow in his dealings with the public is to 11.___

    A. offer aid and cooperation to the public wherever possible
    B. show authority so that the public knows the limits to which they may make requests
    C. ignore the public since the custodian has a specific job to do
    D. refer the public to higher authority for solution of all their problems

12. The students playing in the schoolyard consistently lose rubber balls that land on the school roof. They request that you, the custodian, retrieve these balls
Of the following, the BEST procedure for you to follow is . 12.___

    A. teach them a lesson and refuse to retrieve the balls
    B. retrieve the balls and throw them into the incinerator
    C. one day a week retrieve the balls and return them to the students
    D. retrieve the balls and give them to a local children's charity

13. The president of a charitable organization requests a permit to use the school building. You, the custodian, note that this same organization used the school previously and did not observe the "no smoking" rules.
    The BEST procedure for you to follow is to

    A. deny the organization a permit since they did not obey the school regulations before
    B. issue the permit without any questions since a large group is difficult to control
    C. inform the president that if any of his members continue to disregard the "no smoking" rules, future permits will not be issued
    D. inform the president that if any of his members continue to disregard the "no smoking" rules, you will evict them from the school building

14. Due to some grievances, parents occupy your school on a weekend and refuse to leave. As the school principal is out of town and unavailable, the BEST procedure for you, the custodian on duty, is to

    A. tell your employees to vacate the school
    B. call the police department
    C. cooperate with the parents on the take-over
    D. lock all the people in the school

15. An organization requests a permit to use the school auditorium from the hours of 7 P.M. to 10 P.M. on a Tuesday evening. The organization also requests that its members be allowed to enter the school earlier than 7 P.M. and leave later than 10 P.M.
    The BEST procedure for you, the custodian, to follow is to

    A. inform the organization leader that the organization may only use the school from the hours of 7 P.M. to 10 P.M.
    B. issue the permit without saying anything as you want to maintain good public relations
    C. refer the matter to the school principal as you do not want to get involved
    D. ask the organization leader the reasons for the request and, if the request is fair, issue the permit and let the organization do as it pleases

16. Dog owners in the neighborhood have been disregarding the *curb your dog* signs and walking their dogs on your school lawn. You find that this interferes with the operation of powered lawn mowing equipment.
    Your BEST procedure to follow is to

    A. put up a higher fence
    B. chase the people and dogs away
    C. tell the owners you will call the police department
    D. explain the problem to the owners and ask them to curb their dogs

17. A cleaner reports to the custodian that a particular schoolroom is consistently messy and dirty. The one who is equally at fault as the students for this dirty room is the

    A. students' parents
    B. regular classroom teacher
    C. student peer groups
    D. cleaner for reporting the matter

18. A parent walks into a custodian's office and starts to shout at him about a claimed injustice to her child. The PROPER procedure for the custodian to follow is to

    A. call the police department
    B. summon the security guards
    C. vacate the office
    D. escort the parent to a guidance counselor

19. A newspaper reporter visiting a school should normally be referred to the

    A. school principal
    B. school custodian engineer
    C. assistant superintendent of schools
    D. borough supervisor of school custodians

20. The parents of children in the neighborhood of your school complain to you that their children cannot use the school playground after school hours because the gates are closed. The BEST procedure for you to follow is

    A. tell the parents the gates will remain closed after school hours
    B. arrange for the children to use a play street
    C. tell the parents to meet with the board on this matter
    D. try to arrange for the school gates to be open to a later hour after school hours

21. Assume that there is a regulation requiring the men to notify the custodian when they intend to be absent. One of your men stays out without notifying you.
    Of the following, the FIRST thing that you should do is to

    A. discuss the matter with your supervisor
    B. find out the reason for the man's failure to comply with this regulation
    C. threaten the man with disciplinary action
    D. find out what the other custodians are doing about similar situations

22. The members of a crew are LEAST likely to object to strict rules as long as

    A. they know who made them
    B. the rules are applied only occasionally as a disciplinary measure
    C. the rules are applied equally to all the workers
    D. they are posted in a public place

23. Your supervisor complains to you that he could not find you at your assigned location and that the crew under your supervision was idle while you were away.
    Of the following, it is MOST important for you to

    A. improve your supervisory practices
    B. warn the men to look busy whenever they see one of the bosses
    C. disregard such an unreasonable complaint
    D. make certain you are rarely away from your assigned location

24. Assume that the crew you supervise considers some of their routine work unpleasant. The BEST way to get these unpleasant tasks done is to

    A. rotate them among all your men
    B. assign them to easygoing workers who never complain
    C. use them as a means of disciplining habitual latecomers
    D. do them yourself

25. Assume that when a custodian arrives at a job location, he finds that a loud argument is going on between two of his men.
    Of the following, the MOST advisable action for him to take first is to

    A. send one of the men to another job
    B. find out what caused the argument
    C. ask one of the other men to tell him the cause of the argument
    D. take the men with him to his supervisor

KEY (CORRECT ANSWERS)

1. A
2. B
3. D
4. C
5. A

6. B
7. D
8. C
9. A
10. D

11. A
12. C
13. C
14. B
15. A

16. D
17. B
18. D
19. A
20. D

21. B
22. C
23. A
24. A
25. B

TEST 2

DIRECTIONS: Each question or incomplete statement is followed by several suggested answers or completions. Select the one that BEST answers the question or completes the statement. *PRINT THE LETTER OF THE CORRECT ANSWER IN THE SPACE AT THE RIGHT.*

1. Of the following, the BEST reason for a custodian NOT allowing his employees to accept tips from people is that

    A. all employees would not be given equal treatment
    B. employees would become dishonest
    C. people are entitled to service without tips
    D. people in projects can't afford tips

2. Your attitude as a custodian to complaints by your employees should be that

    A. all employees like to complain
    B. if you let the worker "give off some steam," the complaint will disappear
    C. you will listen to them and try to correct the condition
    D. you will try to show the worker where he is wrong

3. A requisition would be filled out by a custodian in order to

    A. get supplies from the stockroom
    B. return to the stockroom supplies you haven't used
    C. find out the supplies you have on hand
    D. show that supplies were used up faster than expected

4. Assume that you are a custodian and have to write a report on a new employee who will finish his probationary period next month.
Which one of the following would be the BEST reason for recommending that he be dropped from the job? He

    A. was late several times during the past five months for a total of 50 minutes
    B. is a slow worker compared to the other men
    C. insists on eating his lunch alone instead of with the other men
    D. is in the habit of accepting drinks from outsiders during working hours although you have often told him it is forbidden

5. It is MOST important that a report from a custodian to his superior be

    A. typewritten
    B. free of any mistakes in spelling or English
    C. accurate and have all the necessary facts
    D. brief to save time of all concerned

6. Suppose that you are a custodian and one of your men asks why you did not recommend him for an above-average work performance rating.
You should tell him

    A. that above-average work reports can be recommended only by higher authority
    B. why you did not give him an above-average work report
    C. that you will recommend an above-average v/ork performance rating next year if he does better work
    D. how he can appeal his rating and help him write his appeal

7. Suppose that you are a custodian and one of your men is absent from work one day. You don't have any extra men and some of the work usually done by the absent man has to be finished that day.
It would be BEST for you to

   A. call your men together and let them decide which one is to do the work
   B. shorten the lunch period and have each man do some of the work
   C. ask one of your better men to *pitch in* by doing a little extra work today
   D. explain to the buildings superintendent why it will not be possible to finish this work today

8. One of your men complains about a job you gave him. He is angry about getting the assignment. You don't think that the man is right in getting so upset.
You should

   A. discuss the problem with him and explain why you gave him the job
   B. refer the man to your supervisor because he refuses to obey orders
   C. show the man that the whole matter is unimportant and a waste of time
   D. tell the man to do the job first and complain later

9. Two of your men start an argument while at work. As a custodian, you should

   A. ignore them; it is normal for men working together to have arguments
   B. stop them right away and find out what started the argument
   C. let them argue it out as long as they continue working and don't talk too loud
   D. speak to one of the men privately and tell him he is interfering with the work

10. Suppose you are a new custodian and you are put in charge of a crew of men whom you do not know and who have been working together for a few months.
For a smooth changeover to your leadership, it would be BEST for you to

    A. let them continue working at their present assignments while you get to know them better
    B. tell the men to call their old supervisor if they have any trouble while you are learning the job
    C. ask the most experienced man to take charge of the crew for a short while until you are more familiar with the work
    D. ask each man whether he is satisfied with what he is doing or wants a change

11. One of your men makes a suggestion for improving the method of doing the work. You don't think the suggestion is workable.
You should, as a custodian,

    A. forget the idea since it isn't workable
    B. tell the man to try out the idea and hold him responsible if it doesn't work out
    C. discuss with the man why you think the idea won't work and praise him for his interest in the job
    D. point out to the man that he is wasting your time bringing up an idea that is not practical

12. Suppose that you and your supervisor are making an inspection of one of the buildings you are responsible for cleaning. Your superior notices that the elevator in the building has not been cleaned. You know that a new employee who has been on the job for only three months is assigned to this building. You should

    A. tell your supervisor that you will have the elevator cleaned and see that it is kept clean in the future
    B. explain to your supervisor the trouble you have in training new employees
    C. find the new man and ask him to explain to you and your superior why the elevator is not clean
    D. tell your supervisor that the elevator was clean when you made your last inspection

13. Suppose that your men were asked to work overtime in order to repair a water main break. When the work is finished, your superior thanks you for the excellent work that was done.
    For you, a custodian, to tell your men about this would be

    A. *bad,* because this was a private conversation between you and your superior
    B. *good,* because your men will see that you are well-liked by your superior
    C. *bad,* because your men will think that they will be asked to work whenever there is an emergency
    D. *good,* because it will show the men their cooperation is appreciated

14. When you, as a custodian, discuss a grievance with an employee, you should

    A. not tell the employee what you think of his complaint until a later date
    B. avoid any arguments with the employee
    C. convince the employee that there is no basis for this grievance
    D. tell the employee his complaint is justified

15. At a quarter to five, one of your employees tells you that the incinerator in his building has much refuse in it and he is willing to work overtime to burn it.
    If you give him permission to do this, it would be

    A. *good,* because it will save time the next day for other important work
    B. *bad,* because this is not an emergency for which overtime could be approved
    C. *good,* because tenants would not complain that refuse piles up and causes odors
    D. *bad,* because the law does not allow burning after 5:00 P.M.

16. Because of absences, you are left short-handed.
    Which one of the following operations should you lay over so that you can cover the MOST important work on a minimum basis?

    A. Incineration of garbage
    B. Sweeping the lobby
    C. Sweeping and washing the elevators
    D. Washing corridor windows

17. Suppose that one of your men who is doing good work asks for a transfer to another custodian.
It would be BEST for you to

   A. have a private talk with the man to find out why he wants a transfer
   B. tell the man that the other custodian will also expect him to do good work
   C. approve the transfer without question because a dissatisfied man will do a poor job
   D. ask the other men in your crew if they are dissatisfied with your supervision

17._____

18. One of your experienced workers and a new employee are arguing about the correct way to do a job on which they are working together.
As a custodian, you should

   A. listen to both men and then tell them that they must learn to settle their argument without interrupting your work
   B. side with the older worker because he is more experienced
   C. listen to both men and then tell them how the work is to be done
   D. take one of the men off the job

18._____

19. Suppose that the department is introducing a new procedure for cleaning the hallways of buildings.
As a custodian, the BEST way for you to acquaint your men with this new procedure and to get them to use it is to

   A. wait until it has been tried out in another building and, if it is successful, put it into use in your building
   B. give each man a printed copy of the new procedure and set a deadline date by which each man is to read it and know it
   C. get your men together and explain the new procedure to them and how it will affect their work
   D. teach it to your best man and when he is familiar with it, ask him to teach it to the other men one at a time

19._____

20. Suppose that, as a custodian, you have finished *breaking in* a new employee. A few days later, you see the new man doing the job the wrong way.
You should

   A. immediately show the man what he is doing wrong and how to do it correctly
   B. assign him to some other work
   C. let your superior know that the new man cannot follow instructions
   D. say nothing because you may make the new man nervous

20._____

21. Suppose that a new type waxing machine is to be used in your building.
Of the following, the BEST way for you to teach your men how to use this machine is to

   A. give a talk on how to operate the machine
   B. demonstrate the operation and then have each man operate the machine under your supervision
   C. have the manufacturer give a talk on how to operate the machine
   D. give each man a set of carefully written instructions on how to operate the machine

21._____

22. When a custodian has to teach a man a new job, it would be MOST helpful for him to find out

    A. how long the man has been with the department and how long he plans to stay
    B. the man's dependability and willingness
    C. the man's past record of cooperation with other workers
    D. what the man already knows that will help him in learning the new job

23. When a new custodian comes on the job, it is LEAST important for him to know

    A. the location of the buildings in the unit
    B. how long the foremen have been there
    C. the names of the men who work there
    D. where the tools and equipment are kept

24. When you assign work to your men, it is usually BEST to

    A. give each man the same amount of work
    B. give the jobs that take the longest time to the senior men
    C. assign work to each man according to his ability
    D. let each man pick his own assignment

25. As a custodian, you will MOST likely be respected by your men if you

    A. keep your personnel records simple and clear
    B. offer them advice in solving their family problems
    C. leave it to them to decide how a job is to be done
    D. are fair and honest with them

KEY (CORRECT ANSWERS)

1. C
2. C
3. A
4. D
5. C

6. B
7. C
8. A
9. B
10. A

11. C
12. A
13. D
14. B
15. D

16. D
17. A
18. C
19. C
20. A

21. B
22. D
23. B
24. C
25. D

TEST 3

DIRECTIONS: Each question or incomplete statement is followed by several suggested answers or completions. Select the one that BEST answers the question or completes the statement. *PRINT THE LETTER OF THE CORRECT ANSWER IN THE SPACE AT THE RIGHT.*

1. Good public relations can be damaged by a custodian who treats tenants, fellow workers, friends, relatives, and the public with

    A. courtesy
    B. consideration
    C. contempt
    D. respect

    1.___

2. An office worker complains to a custodian that one of the cleaners broke off a branch of a plant which she kept on her desk and that she can identify the cleaner.
The BEST thing for the custodian to do is to

    A. convince her that the plant will grow another branch eventually
    B. make the cleaner apologize and pay for a new plant out of his own pocket
    C. sympathize with the office worker and assure her that he will speak to the cleaner about it
    D. tell her not to bother him about her personal property

    2.___

3. When a new employee reports to a custodian on his first day on the job, the custodian SHOULD

    A. extend a hearty welcome and make the new employee feel welcome
    B. have the man sit and wait for a while before seeing him so that the employee realizes how busy the custodian is
    C. warn him of stern disciplinary action if he is late or absent excessively
    D. tell him he probably will have difficulty doing the work so that he doesn't become overconfident

    3.___

4. The one of the following subjects of a fire prevention training program which is MOST readily applied on the job is the

    A. elimination of fire hazards
    B. use of portable fire extinguishers
    C. knowledge of types of fires
    D. method of reporting fires

    4.___

5. A custodian who is a good supervisor will NOT

    A. tell his men what their jobs are and why they are important
    B. show his men how their jobs are to be done in the right way
    C. require some of the men to do their jobs in the presence of the supervisor demonstrating that they understand the job
    D. leave his men alone because they will always do their jobs correctly once they have received their instructions

    5.___

6. When a custodian sees a worker doing his job incorrectly, he should

    A. tell the worker to be more careful
    B. suspend the worker until he learns to do the job correctly
    C. tell the worker specifically how the job should be done
    D. scold the man

    6.___

7. An employee who is a good worker but is often late for work   7._____

   A. is lazy and should be dismissed
   B. cannot tell time
   C. can have no excuse for being late more than once a month
   D. should be questioned by his supervisor to try to find out why he is late

8. When starting any disciplinary action, a custodian who is a good supervisor should   8._____

   A. show his annoyance by losing his temper
   B. be apologetic
   C. be sarcastic
   D. be firm and positive

9. The BEST way for a custodian to maintain good employee morale is to   9._____

   A. avoid praising any one employee
   B. always have an alibi for his own mistakes
   C. encourage cliques by giving them information before giving it to other workers
   D. give adequate credit and praise when due

10. The BEST way for a custodian to tell if the night cleaners have done their work well is to check   10._____

    A. on how much cleaning material has been used
    B. on how much waste paper was collected
    C. the building for cleanliness
    D. the floor mops to see if they are still wet

11. The one of the following which is the BEST reason for introducing a training program is that the   11._____

    A. quality of work is above standard
    B. employees are all experienced
    C. accident rate is too high
    D. complaints are negligible

12. The FIRST step in training an inexperienced individual in a particular job is to   12._____

    A. put him to work and watch for mistakes
    B. put him to work and tell him to call for help if he needs it
    C. put him at ease and then find out what he knows about the work
    D. tell him to watch the least experienced worker on the job because the training is still fresh in his mind

13. As used in job analysis, the term *job breakdown* means   13._____

    A. any equipment failure
    B. any failure on the part of the worker to complete the job
    C. dividing the job into a series of steps
    D. reducing the number of workers by 50 percent

14. In dealing with the public, a custodian should be

   A. indulgent
   B. courteous
   C. disagreeable
   D. unavailable

15. If a custodian sees a group of people in front of his building preparing to form a picket line, he should

   A. turn on a lawn sprinkler to spray the pickets
   B. order the pickets off the sidewalk in front of the building
   C. show the pickets he is sympathetic with their complaint against the city
   D. contact his supervisor immediately for instructions

16. When electric service in a public building is to be shut off from 10 A.M. Tuesday to 11:30 the next morning because a new electric feeder cable is being installed, the custodian should

   A. prepare a memo to all office supervisors in the building, notifying them of the situation, and deliver a copy to each office as soon as possible
   B. prepare a notice of the impending power stoppage and post it in the lobby early Tuesday morning
   C. tell the electrical contractor to notify the tenants when he is about to shut off the power
   D. discontinue elevator service at 10 A.M. on Tuesday as an indication to the tenants that the power supply is off

17. Time standards for cleaning are of value ONLY if

   A. a bonus is promised if the time standards are beaten
   B. the cleaners determine the methods and procedures to be used
   C. accompanied by a completely detailed description of the methods to be used
   D. a schematic diagram of the area is made available to the cleaners

18. Of the following, the one which is the LEAST important factor in deciding that additional training is necessary for the men you supervise is that

   A. the quality of work is below standard
   B. supplies are being wasted
   C. too much time is required to do specific jobs
   D. the absentee rate has declined

19. To promote proper safety practices in the operation of power tools and equipment, the custodian should emphasize in meetings with his staff that

   A. every accident can be prevented through proper safety regulations
   B. proper safety practices will probably make future safety meetings unnecessary
   C. when safety rules are followed, tools and equipment will work better
   D. safety rules are based on past experience with the best methods of preventing accidents

20. As a custodian, a GOOD practical method to use in determining whether an employee is doing his job properly is to

    A. assume that if he asks no questions, he knows the work
    B. question him directly on details of the job
    C. inspect and follow-up the work which is assigned to him
    D. ask other employees how this employee is making out

21. If an employee continually asks how he should do his work, the custodian should

    A. dismiss him immediately
    B. pretend he does not hear him unless he persists
    C. explain the work carefully but encourage him to use his own judgment
    D. tell him not to ask so many questions

22. As a custodian, you have instructed an employee to wet mop a certain area.
    To be sure that the employee understands the instructions you have given him, you should

    A. ask him to repeat the instructions to you
    B. check with him after he has done the job
    C. watch him while he is doing the job
    D. repeat the instructions to the employee

23. As a custodian, one of your men disagrees with your evaluation of his work.
    Of the following, the BEST way to handle this situation would be to

    A. explain that you are in a better position to evaluate his work than he is
    B. tell him that since the other men are satisfied with your evaluation, he should accept their opinions
    C. explain the basis of your evaluation and discuss it with him
    D. refuse to discuss his complaint in order to maintain discipline

24. Of the following, the one which is NOT a purpose of a cleaning job breakdown is to

    A. eliminate unnecessary steps
    B. determine the type of floor wax to use
    C. rearrange the sequence of operations to save time
    D. combine steps or actions where practicable

25. The BEST method of making cleaning assignments in a large building is by means of

    A. daily rotation
    B. specific assignment
    C. individual choice
    D. chronological order

KEY (CORRECT ANSWERS)

1. C
2. C
3. A
4. A
5. D

6. C
7. D
8. D
9. D
10. C

11. C
12. C
13. C
14. B
15. D

16. A
17. C
18. D
19. D
20. C

21. C
22. A
23. C
24. B
25. B

PHILOSOPHY, PRINCIPLES, PRACTICES, AND TECHNICS
OF
SUPERVISION, ADMINISTRATION, MANAGEMENT, AND ORGANIZATION

TABLE OF CONTENTS

	Page
MEANING OF SUPERVISION	1
THE OLD AND THE NEW SUPERVISION	1
THE EIGHT (8) BASIC PRINCIPLES OF THE NEW SUPERVISION	1
I. Principle of Responsibility	1
II. Principle of Authority	2
III. Principle of Self-Growth	2
IV. Principle of Individual Worth	2
V. Principle of Creative Leadership	2
VI. Principle of Success and Failure	2
VII. Principle of Science	3
VIII. Principle of Cooperation	3
WHAT IS ADMINISTRATION?	3
I. Practices Commonly Classed as "Supervisory"	3
II. Practices Commonly Classed as "Administrative"	3
III. Practices Commonly Classed as Both "Supervisory" and "Administrative"	4
RESPONSIBILITIES OF THE SUPERVISOR	4
COMPETENCIES OF THE SUPERVISOR	4
THE PROFESSIONAL SUPERVISOR-EMPLOYEE RELATIONSHIP	4
MINI-TEXT IN SUPERVISION, ADMINISTRATION, MANAGEMENT, AND ORGANIZATION	5
I. Brief Highlights	5
A. Levels of Management	6
B. What the Supervisor Must Learn	6
C. A Definition of Supervision	6
D. Elements of the Team Concept	6
E. Principles of Organization	6
F. The Four Important Parts of Every Job	7
G. Principles of Delegation	7
H. Principles of Effective Communications	7
I. Principles of Work Improvement	7
J. Areas of Job Improvement	7
K. Seven Key Points in Making Improvements	8

	L.	Corrective Techniques for Job Improvement	8
	M.	A Planning Checklist	8
	N.	Five Characteristics of Good Directions	9
	O.	Types of Directions	9
	P.	Controls	9
	Q.	Orienting the New Employee	9
	R.	Checklist for Orienting New Employees	9
	S.	Principles of Learning	10
	T.	Causes of Poor Performance	10
	U.	Four Major Steps in On-the-Job Instructions	10
	V.	Employees Want Five Things	10
	W.	Some Don'ts in Regard to Praise	11
	X.	How to Gain Your Workers' Confidence	11
	Y.	Sources of Employee Problems	11
	Z.	The Supervisor's Key to Discipline	11
	AA.	Five Important Processes of Management	12
	BB.	When the Supervisor Fails to Plan	12
	CC.	Fourteen General Principles of Management	12
	DD.	Change	12
II.	Brief Topical Summaries		13
	A.	Who/What is the Supervisor?	13
	B.	The Sociology of Work	13
	C.	Principles and Practices of Supervision	14
	D.	Dynamic Leadership	14
	E.	Processes for Solving Problems	15
	F.	Training for Results	15
	G.	Health, Safety, and Accident Prevention	16
	H.	Equal Employment Opportunity	16
	I.	Improving Communications	16
	J.	Self-Development	17
	K.	Teaching and Training	17
		1. The Teaching Process	17
		a. Preparation	17
		b. Presentation	18
		c. Summary	18
		d. Application	18
		e. Evaluation	18
		2. Teaching Methods	18
		a. Lecture	18
		b. Discussion	18
		c. Demonstration	19
		d. Performance	19
		e. Which Method to Use	19

PHILOSOPHY, PRINCIPLES, PRACTICES, AND TECHNICS
OF
SUPERVISION, ADMINISTRATION, MANAGEMENT, AND ORGANIZATION

MEANING OF SUPERVISION

The extension of the democratic philosophy has been accompanied by an extension in the scope of supervision. Modern leaders and supervisors no longer think of supervision in the narrow sense of being confined chiefly to visiting employees, supplying materials, or rating the staff. They regard supervision as being intimately related to all the concerned agencies of society, they speak of the supervisor's function in terms of "growth," rather than the "improvement" of employees.

This modern concept of supervision may be defined as follows: Supervision is leadership and the development of leadership within groups which are cooperatively engaged in inspection, research, training, guidance, and evaluation.

THE OLD AND THE NEW SUPERVISION

TRADITIONAL
1. Inspection
2. Focused on the employee
3. Visitation
4. Random and haphazard
5. Imposed and authoritarian
6. One person usually

MODERN
1. Study and analysis
2. Focused on aims, materials, methods, supervisors, employees, environment
3. Demonstrations, intervisitation, workshops, directed reading, bulletins, etc.
4. Definitely organized and planned (scientific)
5. Cooperative and democratic
6. Many persons involved (creative)

THE EIGHT (8) BASIC PRINCIPLES OF THE NEW SUPERVISION

I. Principle of Responsibility
   Authority to act and responsibility for acting must be joined.
   A. If you give responsibility, give authority.
   B. Define employee duties clearly.
   C. Protect employees from criticism by others.
   D. Recognize the rights as well as obligations of employees.
   E. Achieve the aims of a democratic society insofar as it is possible within the area of your work.
   F. Establish a situation favorable to training and learning.
   G. Accept ultimate responsibility for everything done in your section, unit, office, division, department.
   H. Good administration and good supervision are inseparable.

II. Principle of Authority
The success of the supervisor is measured by the extent to which the power of authority is not used.
   A. Exercise simplicity and informality in supervision
   B. Use the simplest machinery of supervision
   C. If it is good for the organization as a whole, it is probably justified.
   D. Seldom be arbitrary or authoritative.
   E. Do not base your work on the power of position or of personality.
   F. Permit and encourage the free expression of opinions.

III. Principle of Self-Growth
The success of the supervisor is measured by the extent to which, and the speed with which, he is no longer needed.
   A. Base criticism on principles, not on specifics.
   B. Point out higher activities to employees.
   C. Train for self-thinking by employees to meet new situations.
   D. Stimulate initiative, self-reliance, and individual responsibility
   E. Concentrate on stimulating the growth of employees rather than on removing defects.

IV. Principle of Individual Worth
Respect for the individual is a paramount consideration in supervision.
   A. Be human and sympathetic in dealing with employees.
   B. Don't nag about things to be done.
   C. Recognize the individual differences among employees and seek opportunities to permit best expression of each personality.

V. Principle of Creative Leadership
The best supervision is that which is not apparent to the employee.
   A. Stimulate, don't drive employees to creative action.
   B. Emphasize doing good things.
   C. Encourage employees to do what they do best.
   D. Do not be too greatly concerned with details of subject or method.
   E. Do not be concerned exclusively with immediate problems and activities.
   F. Reveal higher activities and make them both desired and maximally possible.
   G. Determine procedures in the light of each situation but see that these are derived from a sound basic philosophy.
   H. Aid, inspire, and lead so as to liberate the creative spirit latent in all good employees.

VI. Principle of Success and Failure
There are no unsuccessful employees, only unsuccessful supervisors who have failed to give proper leadership.
   A. Adapt suggestions to the capacities, attitudes, and prejudices of employees.
   B. Be gradual, be progressive, be persistent.
   C. Help the employee find the general principle; have the employee apply his own problem to the general principle.
   D. Give adequate appreciation for good work and honest effort.
   E. Anticipate employee difficulties and help to prevent them.
   F. Encourage employees to do the desirable things they will do anyway.
   G. Judge your supervision by the results it secures.

VII. Principle of Science
Successful supervision is scientific, objective, and experimental. It is based on facts, not on prejudices.
   A. Be cumulative in results.
   B. Never divorce your suggestions from the goals of training.
   C. Don't be impatient of results.
   D. Keep all matters on a professional, not a personal, level.
   E. Do not be concerned exclusively with immediate problems and activities.
   F. Use objective means of determining achievement and rating where possible.

VIII. Principle of Cooperation
Supervision is a cooperative enterprise between supervisor and employee.
   A. Begin with conditions as they are.
   B. Ask opinions of all involved when formulating policies.
   C. Organization is as good as its weakest link.
   D. Let employees help to determine policies and department programs.
   E. Be approachable and accessible—physically and mentally.
   F. Develop pleasant social relationships.

WHAT IS ADMINISTRATION

Administration is concerned with providing the environment, the material facilities, and the operational procedures that will promote the maximum growth and development of supervisors and employees. (Organization is an aspect and a concomitant of administration.)

There is no sharp line of demarcation between supervision and administration; these functions are intimately interrelated and, often, overlapping. They are complementary activities.

I. Practices Commonly Classed as "Supervisory"
   A. Conducting employees' conferences
   B. Visiting sections, units, offices, divisions, departments
   C. Arranging for demonstrations
   D. Examining plans
   E. Suggesting professional reading
   F. Interpreting bulletins
   G. Recommending in-service training courses
   H. Encouraging experimentation
   I. Appraising employee morale
   J. Providing for intervisitation

II. Practices Commonly Classified as "Administrative"
   A. Management of the office
   B. Arrangement of schedules for extra duties
   C. Assignment of rooms or areas
   D. Distribution of supplies
   E. Keeping records and reports
   F. Care of audio-visual materials
   G. Keeping inventory records
   H. Checking record cards and books

I. Programming special activities
J. Checking on the attendance and punctuality of employees

III. Practices Commonly Classified as Both "Supervisory" and "Administrative"
A. Program construction
B. Testing or evaluating outcomes
C. Personnel accounting
D. Ordering instructional materials

RESPONSIBILITIES OF THE SUPERVISOR

A person employed in a supervisory capacity must constantly be able to improve his own efficiency and ability. He represent the employer to the employees and only continuous self-examination can make him a capable supervisor.

Leadership and training are the supervisor's responsibility. An efficient working unit is one in which the employees work with the supervisor. It is his job to bring out the best in his employees. He must always be relaxed, courteous, and calm in his association with his employees. Their feelings are important, and a harsh attitude does not develop the most efficient employees.

COMPETENCES OF THE SUPERVISOR

I. Complete knowledge of the duties and responsibilities of his position.
II. To be able to organize a job, plan ahead, and carry through.
III. To have self-confidence and initiative.
IV. To be able to handle the unexpected situation and make quick decisions.
V. To be able to properly train subordinates in the positions they are best suited for.
VI. To be able to keep good human relations among his subordinates.
VII. To be able to keep good human relations between his subordinates and himself and to earn their respect and trust.

THE PROFESSIONAL SUPERVISOR-EMPLOYEE RELATIONSHIP

There are two kinds of efficiency: one kind is only apparent and is produced in organizations through the exercise of mere discipline; this is but a simulation of the second, or true, efficiency which springs from spontaneous cooperation. If you are a manager, no matter how great or small your responsibility, it is your job, in the final analysis, to create and develop this involuntary cooperation among the people whom you supervise. For, no matter how powerful a combination of money, machines, and materials a company may have, this is a dead and sterile thing without a team of willing, thinking, and articulate people to guide it.

The following 21 points are presented as indicative of the exemplary basic relationship that should exist between supervisor and employee:

1. Each person wants to be liked and respected by his fellow employee and wants to be treated with consideration and respect by his superior.
2. The most competent employee will make an error. However, in a unit where good relations exist between the supervisor and his employees, tenseness and fear do not exist. Thus, errors are not hidden or covered up, and the efficiency of a unit is not impaired.

3. Subordinates resent rules, regulations, or orders that are unreasonable or unexplained.
4. Subordinates are quick to resent unfairness, harshness, injustices, and favoritism.
5. An employee will accept responsibility if he knows that he will be complimented for a job well done, and not too harshly chastised for failure; that his supervisor will check the cause of the failure, and, if it was the supervisor's fault, he will assume the blame therefore. If it was the employee's fault, his supervisor will explain the correct method or means of handling the responsibility.
6. An employee wants to receive credit for a suggestion he has made, that is used. If a suggestion cannot be used, the employee is entitled to an explanation. The supervisor should not say "no" and close the subject.
7. Fear and worry slow up a worker's ability. Poor working environment can impair his physical and mental health. A good supervisor avoids forceful methods, threats, and arguments to get a job done.
8. A forceful supervisor is able to train his employees individually and as a team, and is able to motivate them in the proper channels.
9. A mature supervisor is able to properly evaluate his subordinates and to keep them happy and satisfied.
10. A sensitive supervisor will never patronize his subordinates.
11. A worthy supervisor will respect his employees' confidences.
12. Definite and clear-cut responsibilities should be assigned to each executive.
13. Responsibility should always be coupled with corresponding authority.
14. No change should be made in the scope or responsibilities of a position without a definite understanding to that effect on the part of all persons concerned.
15. No executive or employee, occupying a single position in the organization, should be subject to definite orders from more than one source.
16. Orders should never be given to subordinates over the head of a responsible executive. Rather than do this, the officer in question should be supplanted.
17. Criticisms of subordinates should, whoever possible, be made privately, and in no case should a subordinate be criticized in the presence of executives or employees of equal or lower rank.
18. No dispute or difference between executives or employees as to authority or responsibilities should be considered too trivial for prompt and careful adjudication.
19. Promotions, wage changes, and disciplinary action should always be approved by the executive immediately superior to the one directly responsible.
20. No executive or employee should ever be required, or expected, to be at the same time an assistant to, and critic of, another.
21. Any executive whose work is subject to regular inspection should, wherever practicable, be given the assistance and facilities necessary to enable him to maintain an independent check of the quality of his work.

MINI-TEXT IN SUPERVISION, ADMINISTRATION, MANAGEMENT, AND ORGANIZATION

I. Brief Highlights

Listed concisely and sequentially are major headings and important data in the field for quick recall and review.

A. Levels of Management
Any organization of some size has several levels of management. In terms of a ladder, the levels are:

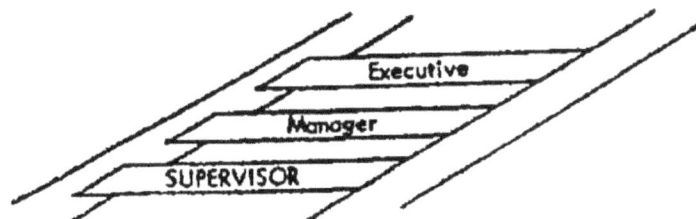

The first level is very important because it is the beginning point of management leadership.

B. What the Supervisor Must Learn
A supervisor must learn to:
1. Deal with people and their differences
2. Get the job done through people
3. Recognize the problems when they exist
4. Overcome obstacles to good performance
5. Evaluate the performance of people
6. Check his own performance in terms of accomplishment

C. A Definition of Supervisor
The term supervisor means any individual having authority, in the interests of the employer, to hire, transfer, suspend, lay-off, recall, promote, discharge, assign, reward, or discipline other employees or responsibility to direct them, or to adjust their grievances, or effectively to recommend such action, if, in connection with the foregoing, exercise of such authority is not of a merely routine or clerical nature but requires the use of independent judgment.

D. Elements of the Team Concept
What is involved in teamwork? The component parts are:
1. Members
2. A leader
3. Goals
4. Plans
5. Cooperation
6. Spirit

E. Principles of Organization
1. A team member must know what his job is.
2. Be sure that the nature and scope of a job are understood.
3. Authority and responsibility should be carefully spelled out.
4. A supervisor should be permitted to make the maximum number of decisions affecting his employees.
5. Employees should report to only one supervisor.
6. A supervisor should direct only as many employees as he can handle effectively.
7. An organization plan should be flexible.

8. Inspection and performance of work should be separate.
9. Organizational problems should receive immediate attention.
10. Assign work in line with ability and experience.

F. The Four Important Parts of Every Job
1. Inherent in every job is the *accountability* for results.
2. A second set of factors in every job is *responsibilities*.
3. Along with duties and responsibilities one must have the *authority* to act within certain limits without obtaining permission to proceed.
4. No job exists in a vacuum. The supervisor is surrounded by key *relationships*.

G. Principles of Delegation
Where work is delegated for the first time, the supervisor should think in terms of these questions:
1. Who is best qualified to do this?
2. Can an employee improve his abilities by doing this?
3. How long should an employee spend on this?
4. Are there any special problems for which he will need guidance?
5. How broad a delegation can I make?

H. Principles of Effective Communications
1. Determine the media.
2. To whom directed?
3. Identification and source authority.
4. Is communication understood?

I. Principles of Work Improvement
1. Most people usually do only the work which is assigned to them.
2. Workers are likely to fit assigned work into the time available to perform it.
3. A good workload usually stimulates output.
4. People usually do their best work when they know that results will be reviewed or inspected.
5. Employees usually feel that someone else is responsible for conditions of work, workplace layout, job methods, type of tools/equipment, and other such factors.
6. Employees are usually defensive about their job security.
7. Employees have natural resistance to change.
8. Employees can support or destroy a supervisor.
9. A supervisor usually earns the respect of his people through his personal example of diligence and efficiency.

J. Areas of Job Improvement
The areas of job improvement are quite numerous, but the most common ones which a supervisor can identify and utilize are:
1. Departmental layout
2. Flow of work
3. Workplace layout
4. Utilization of manpower
5. Work methods
6. Materials handling

7. Utilization
8. Motion economy

K. Seven Key Points in Making Improvements
1. Select the job to be improved
2. Study how it is being done now
3. Question the present method
4. Determine actions to be taken
5. Chart proposed method
6. Get approval and apply
7. Solicit worker participation

L. Corrective Techniques of Job Improvement
Specific Problems
1. Size of workload
2. Inability to meet schedules
3. Strain and fatigue
4. Improper use of men and skills
5. Waste, poor quality, unsafe conditions
6. Bottleneck conditions that hinder output
7. Poor utilization of equipment and machine
8. Efficiency and productivity of labor

General Improvement
1. Departmental layout
2. Flow of work
3. Work plan layout
4. Utilization of manpower
5. Work methods
6. Materials handling
7. Utilization of equipment
8. Motion economy

Corrective Techniques
1. Study with scale model
2. Flow chart study
3. Motion analysis
4. Comparison of units produced to standard allowance
5. Methods analysis
6. Flow chart and equipment study
7. Down time vs. running time
8. Motion analysis

M. A Planning Checklist
1. Objectives
2. Controls
3. Delegations
4. Communications
5. Resources
6. Manpower

7. Equipment
8. Supplies and materials
9. Utilization of time
10. Safety
11. Money
12. Work
13. Timing of improvements

N. Five Characteristics of Good Directions
In order to get results, directions must be:
1. Possible of accomplishment
2. Agreeable with worker interests
3. Related to mission
4. Planned and complete
5. Unmistakably clear

O. Types of Directions
1. Demands or direct orders
2. Requests
3. Suggestion or implication
4. volunteering

P. Controls
A typical listing of the overall areas in which the supervisor should establish controls might be:
1. Manpower
2. Materials
3. Quality of work
4. Quantity of work
5. Time
6. Space
7. Money
8. Methods

Q. Orienting the New Employee
1. Prepare for him
2. Welcome the new employee
3. Orientation for the job
4. Follow-up

R. Checklist for Orienting New Employees   Yes   No
1. Do you appreciate the feelings of new employees
   when they first report for work?   ___   ___
2. Are you aware of the fact that the new employee must
   make a big adjustment to his job?   ___   ___
3. Have you given him good reasons for liking the job and
   the organization?   ___   ___
4. Have you prepared for his first day on the job?   ___   ___
5. Did you welcome him cordially and make him feel needed?   ___   ___

		Yes	No
6.	Did you establish rapport with him so that he feels free to talk and discuss matters with you?	___	___
7.	Did you explain his job to him and his relationship to you?	___	___
8.	Does he know that his work will be evaluated periodically on a basis that is fair and objective?	___	___
9.	Did you introduce him to his fellow workers in such a way that they are likely to accept him?	___	___
10.	Does he know what employee benefits he will receive?	___	___
11.	Does he understand the importance of being on the job and what to do if he must leave his duty station?	___	___
12.	Has he been impressed with the importance of accident prevention and safe practice?	___	___
13.	Does he generally know his way around the department?	___	___
14.	Is he under the guidance of a sponsor who will teach the right way of doing things?	___	___
15.	Do you plan to follow-up so that he will continue to adjust successfully to his job?	___	___

S. Principles of Learning
1. Motivation
2. Demonstration or explanation
3. Practice

T. Causes of Poor Performance
1. Improper training for job
2. Wrong tools
3. Inadequate directions
4. Lack of supervisory follow-up
5. Poor communications
6. Lack of standards of performance
7. Wrong work habits
8. Low morale
9. Other

U. Four Major Steps in On-The-Job Instruction
1. Prepare the worker
2. Present the operation
3. Tryout performance
4. Follow-up

V. Employees Want Five Things
1. Security
2. Opportunity
3. Recognition
4. Inclusion
5. Expression

W. Some Don'ts in Regard to Praise
   1. Don't praise a person for something he hasn't done.
   2. Don't praise a person unless you can be sincere.
   3. Don't be sparing in praise just because your superior withholds it from you.
   4. Don't let too much time elapse between good performance and recognition of it

X. How to Gain Your Workers' Confidence
   Methods of developing confidence include such things as:
   1. Knowing the interests, habits, hobbies of employees
   2. Admitting your own inadequacies
   3. Sharing and telling of confidence in others
   4. Supporting people when they are in trouble
   5. Delegating matters that can be well handled
   6. Being frank and straightforward about problems and working conditions
   7. Encouraging others to bring their problems to you
   8. Taking action on problems which impede worker progress

Y. Sources of Employee Problems
   On-the-job causes might be such things as:
   1. A feeling that favoritism is exercised in assignments
   2. Assignment of overtime
   3. An undue amount of supervision
   4. Changing methods or systems
   5. Stealing of ideas or trade secrets
   6. Lack of interest in job
   7. Threat of reduction in force
   8. Ignorance or lack of communications
   9. Poor equipment
   10. Lack of knowing how supervisor feels toward employee
   11. Shift assignments

   Off-the-job problems might have to do with:
   1. Health
   2. Finances
   3. Housing
   4. Family

Z. The Supervisor's Key to Discipline
   There are several key points about discipline which the supervisor should keep in mind:
   1. Job discipline is one of the disciplines of life and is directed by the supervisor.
   2. It is more important to correct an employee fault than to fix blame for it.
   3. Employee performance is affected by problems both on the job and off.
   4. Sudden or abrupt changes in behavior can be indications of important employee problems.
   5. Problems should be dealt with as soon as possible after they are identified.
   6. The attitude of the supervisor may have more to do with solving problems than the techniques of problem solving.
   7. Correction of employee behavior should be resorted to only after the supervisor is sure that training or counseling will not be helpful.

8. Be sure to document your disciplinary actions.
9. Make sure that you are disciplining on the basis of facts rather than personal feelings.
10. Take each disciplinary step in order, being careful not to make snap judgments, or decisions based on impatience.

AA. Five Important Processes of Management
1. Planning
2. Organizing
3. Scheduling
4. Controlling
5. Motivating

BB. When the Supervisor Fails to Plan
1. Supervisor creates impression of not knowing his job
2. May lead to excessive overtime
3. Job runs itself—supervisor lacks control
4. Deadlines and appointments missed
5. Parts of the work go undone
6. Work interrupted by emergencies
7. Sets a bad example
8. Uneven workload creates peaks and valleys
9. Too much time on minor details at expense of more important tasks

CC. Fourteen General Principles of Management
1. Division of work
2. Authority and responsibility
3. Discipline
4. Unity of command
5. Unity of direction
6. Subordination of individual interest to general interest
7. Remuneration of personnel
8. Centralization
9. Scalar chain
10. Order
11. Equity
12. Stability of tenure of personnel
13. Initiative
14. Esprit de corps

DD. Change

Bringing about change is perhaps attempted more often, and yet less well understood, than anything else the supervisor does. How do people generally react to change? (People tend to resist change that is imposed upon them by other individuals or circumstances.

Change is characteristic of every situation. It is a part of every real endeavor where the efforts of people are concerned.

1. Why do people resist change?
   People may resist change because of:
   a. Fear of the unknown
   b. Implied criticism
   c. Unpleasant experiences in the past
   d. Fear of loss of status
   e. Threat to the ego
   f. Fear of loss of economic stability

2. How can we best overcome the resistance to change?
   In initiating change, take these steps:
   a. Get ready to sell
   b. Identify sources of help
   c. Anticipate objections
   d. Sell benefits
   e. Listen in depth
   f. Follow up

II. Brief Topical Summaries

   A. Who/What is the Supervisor?
      1. The supervisor is often called the "highest level employee and the lowest level manager."
      2. A supervisor is a member of both management and the work group. He acts as a bridge between the two.
      3. Most problems in supervision are in the area of human relations, or people problems.
      4. Employees expect: Respect, opportunity to learn and to advance, and a sense of belonging, and so forth.
      5. Supervisors are responsible for directing people and organizing work. Planning is of paramount importance.
      6. A position description is a set of duties and responsibilities inherent to a given position.
      7. It is important to keep the position description up-to-date and to provide each employee with his own copy.

   B. The Sociology of Work
      1. People are alike in many ways; however, each individual is unique.
      2. The supervisor is challenged in getting to know employee differences. Acquiring skills in evaluating individuals is an asset.
      3. Maintaining meaningful working relationships in the organization is of great importance.
      4. The supervisor has an obligation to help individuals to develop to their fullest potential.
      5. Job rotation on a planned basis helps to build versatility and to maintain interest and enthusiasm in work groups.
      6. Cross training (job rotation) provides backup skills.

7. The supervisor can help reduce tension by maintaining a sense of humor, providing guidance to employees, and by making reasonable and timely decisions. Employees respond favorably to working under reasonably predictable circumstances.
8. Change is characteristic of all managerial behavior. The supervisor must adjust to changes in procedures, new methods, technological changes, and to a number of new and sometimes challenging situations.
9. To overcome the natural tendency for people to resist change, the supervisor should become more skillful in initiating change.

C. Principles and Practices of Supervision
1. Employees should be required to answer to only one superior.
2. A supervisor can effectively direct only a limited number of employees, depending upon the complexity, variety, and proximity of the jobs involved.
3. The organizational chart presents the organization in graphic form. It reflects lines of authority and responsibility as well as interrelationships of units within the organization.
4. Distribution of work can be improved through an analysis using the "Work Distribution Chart."
5. The "Work Distribution Chart" reflects the division of work within a unit in understandable form.
6. When related tasks are given to an employee, he has a better chance of increasing his skills through training.
7. The individual who is given the responsibility for tasks must also be given the appropriate authority to insure adequate results.
8. The supervisor should delegate repetitive, routine work. Preparation of recurring reports, maintaining leave and attendance records are some examples.
9. Good discipline is essential to good task performance. Discipline is reflected in the actions of employees on the job in the absence of supervision.
10. Disciplinary action may have to be taken when the positive aspects of discipline have failed. Reprimand, warning, and suspension are examples of disciplinary action.
11. If a situation calls for a reprimand, be sure it is deserved and remember it is to be done in private.

D. Dynamic Leadership
1. A style is a personal method or manner of exerting influence.
2. Authoritarian leaders often see themselves as the source of power and authority.
3. The democratic leader often perceives the group as the source of authority and power.
4. Supervisors tend to do better when using the pattern of leadership that is most natural for them.
5. Social scientists suggest that the effective supervisor use the leadership style that best fits the problem or circumstances involved.
6. All four styles—telling, selling, consulting, joining—have their place. Using one does not preclude using the other at another time.

7. The theory X point of view assumes that the average person dislikes work, will avoid it whenever possible, and must be coerced to achieve organizational objectives.
8. The theory Y point of view assumes that the average person considers work to be a natural as play, and, when the individual is committed, he requires little supervision or direction to accomplish desired objectives.
9. The leader's basic assumptions concerning human behavior and human nature affect his actions, decisions, and other managerial practices.
10. Dissatisfaction among employees is often present, but difficult to isolate. The supervisor should seek to weaken dissatisfaction by keeping promises, being sincere and considerate, keeping employees informed, and so forth.
11. Constructive suggestions should be encouraged during the natural progress of the work.

E. Processes for Solving Problems
1. People find their daily tasks more meaningful and satisfying when they can improve them.
2. The causes of problems, or the key factors, are often hidden in the background. Ability to solve problems often involves the ability to isolate them from their backgrounds. There is some substance to the cliché that some persons "can't see the forest for the trees."
3. New procedures are often developed from old ones. Problems should be broken down into manageable parts. New ideas can be adapted from old one.
4. People think differently in problem-solving situations. Using a logical, patterned approach is often useful. One approach found to be useful includes these steps:
   a. Define the problem
   b. Establish objectives
   c. Get the facts
   d. Weigh and decide
   e. Take action
   f. Evaluate action

F. Training for Results
1. Participants respond best when they feel training is important to them.
2. The supervisor has responsibility for the training and development of those who report to him.
3. When training is delegated to others, great care must be exercised to insure the trainer has knowledge, aptitude, and interest for his work as a trainer.
4. Training (learning) of some type goes on continually. The most successful supervisor makes certain the learning contributes in a productive manner to operational goals.
5. New employees are particularly susceptible to training. Older employees facing new job situations require specific training, as well as having need for development and growth opportunities.
6. Training needs require continuous monitoring.
7. The training officer of an agency is a professional with a responsibility to assist supervisors in solving training problems.

8. Many of the self-development steps important to the supervisor's own growth are equally important to the development of peers and subordinates. Knowledge of these is important when the supervisor consults with others on development and growth opportunities.

G. Health, Safety, and Accident Prevention
1. Management-minded supervisors take appropriate measures to assist employees in maintaining health and in assuring safe practices in the work environment.
2. Effective safety training and practices help to avoid injury and accidents.
3. Safety should be a management goal. All infractions of safety which are observed should be corrected without exception.
4. Employees' safety attitude, training and instruction, provision of safe tools and equipment, supervision, and leadership are considered highly important factors which contribute to safety and which can be influenced directly by supervisors.
5. When accidents do occur, they should be investigated promptly for very important reasons, including the fact that information which is gained can be used to prevent accidents in the future.

H. Equal Employment Opportunity
1. The supervisor should endeavor to treat all employees fairly, without regard to religion, race, sex, or national origin.
2. Groups tend to reflect the attitude of the leader. Prejudice can be detected even in very subtle form. Supervisors must strive to create a feeling of mutual respect and confidence in every employee.
3. Complete utilization of all human resources is a national goal. Equitable consideration should be accorded women in the work force, minority-group members, the physically and mentally handicapped, and the older employee. The important question is: "Who can do the job?"
4. Training opportunities, recognition for performance, overtime assignments, promotional opportunities, and all other personnel actions are to be handled on an equitable basis.

I. Improving Communications
1. Communications is achieving understanding between the sender and the receiver of a message. It also means sharing information—the creation of understanding.
2. Communication is basic to all human activity. Words are means of conveying meanings; however, real meanings are in people.
3. There are very practical differences in the effectiveness of one-way, impersonal, and two-way communications. Words spoken face-to-face are better understood. Telephone conversations are effective, but lack the rapport of person-to-person exchanges. The whole person communicates.
4. Cooperation and communication in an organization go hand in hand. When there is a mutual respect between people, spelling out rules and procedures for communicating is unnecessary.
5. There are several barriers to effective communications. These include failure to listen with respect and understanding, lack of skill in feedback, and misinterpreting the meanings of words used by the speaker. It is also common

practice to listen to what we want to hear, and tune out things we do not want to hear.
6. Communication is management's chief problem. The supervisor should accept the challenge to communicate more effectively and to improve interagency and intra-agency communications.
7. The supervisor may often plan for and conduct meetings. The planning phase is critical and may determine the success or the failure of a meeting.
8. Speaking before groups usually requires extra effort. Stage fright may never disappear completely, but it can be controlled.

J. Self-Development
1. Every employee is responsible for his own self-development.
2. Toastmaster and toastmistress clubs offer opportunities to improve skills in oral communications.
3. Planning for one's own self-development is of vital importance. Supervisors know their own strengths and limitations better than anyone else.
4. Many opportunities are open to aid the supervisor in his developmental efforts, including job assignments; training opportunities, both governmental and non-governmental—to include universities and professional conferences and seminars.
5. Programmed instruction offers a means of studying at one's own rate.
6. Where difficulties may arise from a supervisor's being away from his work for training, he may participate in televised home study or correspondence courses to meet his self-development needs.

K. Teaching and Training
1. The Teaching Process
Teaching is encouraging and guiding the learning activities of students toward established goals. In most cases this process consists of five steps: preparation, presentation, summarization, evaluation, and application.

   a. Preparation
   Preparation is two-fold in nature; that of the supervisor and the employee. Preparation by the supervisor is absolutely essential to success. He must know what, when, where, how, and whom he will teach. Some of the factors that should be considered are:
   1) The objectives
   2) The materials needed
   3) The methods to be used
   4) Employee participation
   5) Employee interest
   6) Training aids
   7) Evaluation
   8) Summarization

   Employee preparation consists in preparing the employee to receive the material. Probably the most important single factor in the preparation of the employee is arousing and maintaining his interest. He must know the objectives of the training, why he is there, how the material can be used, and its importance to him.

b. Presentation
In presentation, have a carefully designed plan and follow it. The plan should be accurate and complete, yet flexible enough to meet situations as they arise. The method of presentation will be determined by the particular situation and objectives.

c. Summary
A summary should be made at the end of every training unit and program. In addition, there may be internal summaries depending on the nature of the material being taught. The important thing is that the trainee must always be able to understand how each part of the new material relates to the whole.

d. Application
The supervisor must arrange work so the employee will be given a chance to apply new knowledge or skills while the material is still clear in his mind and interest is high. The trainee does not really know whether he has learned the material until he has been given a chance to apply it. If the material is not applied, it loses most of its value.

e. Evaluation
The purpose of all training is to promote learning. To determine whether the training has been a success or failure, the supervisor must evaluate this learning.
In the broadest sense, evaluation includes all the devices, methods, skills, and techniques used by the supervisor to keep himself and the employees informed as to their progress toward the objectives they are pursuing. The extent to which the employee has mastered the knowledge, skills, and abilities, or changed his attitudes, as determined by the program objectives, is the extent to which instruction has succeeded or failed.
Evaluation should not be confined to the end of the lesson, day, or program but should be used continuously. We shall note later the way this relates to the rest of the teaching process.

2. Teaching Methods
A teaching method is a pattern of identifiable student and instructor activity used in presenting training material.
All supervisors are faced with the problem of deciding which method should be used at a given time.

a. Lecture
The lecture is direct oral presentation of material by the supervisor. The present trend is to place less emphasis on the trainer's activity and more on that of the trainee.

b. Discussion
Teaching by discussion or conference involves using questions and other techniques to arouse interest and focus attention upon certain areas, and by doing so creating a learning situation. This can be one of the most

valuable methods because it gives the employees an opportunity to express their ideas and pool their knowledge.

    c. Demonstration

    The demonstration is used to teach how something works or how to do something. It can be used to show a principle or what the results of a series of actions will be. A well-staged demonstration is particularly effective because it shows proper methods of performance in a realistic manner.

    d. Performance

    Performance is one of the most fundamental of all learning techniques or teaching methods. The trainee may be able to tell how a specific operation should be performed but he cannot be sure he knows how to perform the operation until he has done so.
    As with all methods, there are certain advantages and disadvantages to each method.

    e. Which Method to Use

    Moreover, there are other methods and techniques of teaching. It is difficult to use any method without other methods entering into it. In any learning situation, a combination of methods is usually more effective than any one method alone.

Finally, evaluation must be integrated into the other aspects of the teaching-learning process.

It must be used in the motivation of the trainees; it must be used to assist in developing understanding during the training; and it must be related to employee application of the results of training.

This is distinctly the role of the supervisor.

www.ingramcontent.com/pod-product-compliance
Lightning Source LLC
Chambersburg PA
CBHW081818300426
44116CB00014B/2410